GARDEN GROVE

A History of the Big Strawberry

JIM TORTOLANO

THE History PRESS

Published by The History Press
Charleston, SC 29403
www.historypress.net

Front cover, bottom: Photograph by David Smithson. *Courtesy of the Garden Grove Strawberry Festival Association.*

First published 2015

ISBN 978.1.5402.1271.9

Library of Congress Control Number applied for

Notice: The information in this book is true and complete to the best of our knowledge. It is offered without guarantee on the part of the author or The History Press. The author and The History Press disclaim all liability in connection with the use of this book.

CONTENTS

ACKNOWLEDGEMENTS

Just as there are really no "solo" albums, there are no solo books. The list of people who deserve credit here is so long that if I don't leave some people out, I'll never get past the acknowledgements.

So—with apologies for omissions—here are some thanks to:

My father and mother, Sal and Sadie, who moved me to Garden Grove when I was seven and therefore planted me and the seeds of this book.

The *Orange County Evening News* (1956–70), the lost, lamented daily newspaper that once made Garden Grove seem like the center of the universe to me.

Garden Grove Historical Society, which provided much of the source material for this book. Special thanks to Terry Thomas andJoAnn Thomas.

The City of Garden Grove City Clerk's office.

Marge Swenson, who fired my interest in local history.

Jon Hall, the writer who did much of the research of the more interesting parts of the book while writing for the *Garden Grove Journal*.

Bob and Carol Lewis, the best in-laws anyone could ever hope to have—and darned good workers, too.

Lollie Beauchamp and her late husband, Bruce, both local historians par excellence.

And most of all, to my beautiful and beloved wife, Marilyn Lewis Tortolano, my cherished and spunky partner, without whom this book and my happiness never would have materialized.

INTRODUCTION

American cities, perhaps more so than communities elsewhere, are always in the process of becoming. Crossroads become villages, which turn into towns and then cities.

Once a city, an area then goes through further waves of change as its economy, population and culture shift—and sometimes decline. How American cities facing maturity adapt to the unknown and unknowable vistas of the twenty-first century is a concern for the nine-tenths of the nation's population who live in urban and suburban areas.

To find an example of a community that has grown up with America's westward movement, I didn't have to look very far. Since 1960, I've lived in Garden Grove, a city whose origins predate Custer's Last Stand and whose development has been buffeted—and sometimes benefitted—by wars, earthquakes, economic upheaval, flood and social change.

Garden Grove, population 175,000 or so, is the classic urban or exurban community that came of age in the post–World War II boom. Over a half century later, it's what city-watchers call a "mature suburb," which means that the houses are getting older and the prospects are in flux.

It's true than many such places seem to have a half-life of about a generation or two before settling into decline. It's also true that with enough vigor, vision and good fortune, such a city can blossom and become more than its citizens ever dared dream.

Millions of Americans live (or soon will live) in towns and cities approaching and crossing that fateful dividing line between new and "used," if you will. How we renew our suburbs is already a major issue in this first quarter of the twenty-first century, as it must be, unless we intend to someday start leveling all the national forests and start building townhouses on the Sierra Nevada.

In a sense, then, Garden Grove and cities like it are the final step in the settling of the West. As Don Henley wrote in the celebrated Eagles song "Last Resort": "There is no more new frontier / We have got to make it here."

How one community—my Garden Grove—got to where it is and how it plans to make its future greater than its past is the subject of this book. I believe that many lessons can be learned from how the "City of Youth and Ambition" slumbered, grew, stalled and then grew again.

This is not, as you will soon discover, an entirely dispassionate account of Garden Grove's history. While some journalistic effort has been made to present differing sides of controversies, it's hard to set aside your affection for a place. Someone once said, "You can't really understand something unless you love it." It's not the largest city around, but as a community with lots of heart and soul, I think of it as "The Big Strawberry."

Love of place, love of country and love of your family and yourself are all healthy expressions of a need to belong. It's a human trait, social animals that we are. There are certainly more exotic places in the world than Garden Grove, California, but home being where the heart is, it's what I understand the best.

Chapter 1

THE PLAINS

Somewhere in the great western steppes of America, maybe out Colorado or New Mexico way, you can stand in the knee-high mustard grass and see forever. Stretching to the mountains on the far horizon to the hazy slopes of distant blue-green hills is the great plain that defines so much of the West.

You have to go a distance these days to be in a place where you can imagine what the coastal flatlands of Southern California looked like before the white man and the railroads and orchardman and the subdivider.

Oceans of wavy grass swirled around the occasional olive tree or cactus bush. The only footsteps were the soft padding of a coyote, the skittering of a lizard or the careful tread of wandering Indians moving from one temporary camp to another.

This is what the area now known as Garden Grove was like before its history began to write itself into tax rolls and county records and newspapers: a wide, grassy plain between the river and the mountains to the east and the swampy marshlands to the south.

The flatness of the land, with its light, sandy soil, would define the community for almost all of its story. The level contours made it ideal first for cattle grazing and then for farming and fruit-growing. More recently, its tabletop topography made it among the easiest to turn into the housing tracts that transformed Orange County in the 1950s and '60s.

The intruding hand of the greater world first enters the Garden Grove story in 1784. For years, much of Alta California was just another promising but uncharted wilderness under the dominion of the faraway king of Spain. A mission had been established in 1776 at San Juan Capistrano, but the reach of "civilization" was short and tenuous.

It was in 1784 that Don Pedro Fages, governor of the province, issued a land grant—later confirmed by King Carlos III—to Don Manuel Nieto for the Rancho Las Bolsas. Most of what would eventually become Garden Grove is on the old Las Bolsas grant; a small slice of the western portion of the city came within the boundaries of Rancho Los Coyotes.

The chief feature of the land, aside from its grassy flatness, was the water. The southern part of the region is peppered with artesian wells on a land with a high water table, a situation that still provides much of the community's hydration needs. Also, to the east was the Santa Ana River, the course of which ran then in a more informal manner than it does today.

A modern observer might wonder just where the river would be, considering that—eleven months out of twelve—it appears to be a giant (dry) concrete ditch better suited for skateboarding than rafting. But the Santa Ana River was not always so well contained or well behaved, and the periodic flooding that accompanied the rainy seasons carved multiple channels, one of which ran through what is now Garden Grove.

Had the meandering river of Saint Anne not perambulated farther east to its present course, the history—and perhaps the name—of Garden Grove might have been different. But the same unseen hand of nature that raised the plain from millions of years of sleep as an ocean bed also propelled the area onto its new path as a home for many men and women.

Life on the land passed without much incident for the next fifty years, a home for cattle and the vaqueros who tended them. The land passed from Spain to Mexico to the United States, but circumstances did not change much with the changing of the flags. It took something greater—almost biblical—to end the long, languid heyday of the ranchos.

By 1860, Yankee trader Abel Stearns had acquired much of the original land grants at bargain prices. A New Englander by birth, he came to California in 1828 from Mexico and established himself in Los Angeles. Married to the daughter of a wealthy rancher, Stearns fit himself into the Californio lifestyle that he—and nature—would have a large role in ending.

What he did was approach the second-generation owners of the land grants and begin to buy up the titles, taking control of huge swaths of land that are now worth many billions of dollars. Grasslands and scrub desert that they were at the time, it would have taken a mighty imagination to see neighborhoods and roads and millions of people.

Abel Stearns, a pioneer in the early development of what became Orange County. *Wikimedia Commons.*

Stearns's cattle heaven soon ended, though. On Christmas Eve of 1861, the rains came, and they washed away the old ranchos forever. The downpour was nearly continuous for thirty days, and the Santa Ana River overflowed and spread for miles in every direction.

Thousands of head of cattle were destroyed, and many of the few buildings then established in the Santa Ana Valley were awash or underwater. The area then promptly went from feast to famine as the floods were followed by years of drought, killing off what remained of the great cattle herds.

Many a wealthy landowner was wealthy no more. Stearns himself was forced to sell his interest in the Los Alamitos grant for $31,000, which works out to $1.10 per acre.

What remained of his empire was then sold in 1868 to a syndicate led by Alfred Robinson. Stearns died three years later, but his name lived on in the Stearns Ranchos Company. Today, he is remembered chiefly as the man after whom Stearns Street in Long Beach is named.

This was the end of the era when the land was used for cattle grazing and where man was no more than a visitor. The next phase was coming, bringing the first drumbeats of a now-familiar echo of subdivision, development, boom and bust. With the death of the ranchos, the birth of Garden Grove was just over the next horizon.

Chapter 2

COOK'S TOUR

In Garden Grove, Alonzo Gerry Cook is granted the status of founder of the community—father of his municipal country, as it were. An elementary school is named after him. There's a giant photo of him hanging in city hall and a bronze statue in Civic Center Park. He looks a little surprised at all the fuss he's kicked up.

But like a lot of city founders in the post-cattle era of what would become Orange County, Cook was more of a speculator than he was a community builder. He spent only about six years in Garden Grove, and claims that he established the community and invented its name are open to considerable variation of opinion.

There is also some confusion over just when the village was started, although 1874 is usually given as the year. It is certainly true that other American families preceded Cook to the area that would become Garden Grove and that there were settlers here as early as 1869, by some accounts.

Records and memories are sketchy, but the best information has John Mitchell as the first permanent settler in Garden Grove, arriving sometime in the late 1860s and securing a deed to an eighty-acre site at what is now the southwest corner of Cannery Road and Garden Grove Boulevard, quite a distance from the town site that would spring up around what's now called Main Street.

Other families followed, and small clusters of homes and farms began to dot the landscape. If Cook was not the literal pioneer of the community, he was certainly the man who helped give it a focus.

Alonzo Gerry Cook, founder of Garden Grove. *Garden Grove Historical Society.*

Cook was probably born in 1842, although some sources state 1839. "Probably" is a good word to employ heavily in this time and place, as identities, ages and addresses had a way of shifting under pressure in the Old West.

Garden Grove's titular founder has been variously described as a medical doctor, an attorney, a farmer and what would certainly today be considered a developer. Cook ran for the California State Assembly and reportedly worked as a probate judge in Idaho and a government attorney in Washington State, both territories at the time.

What brought Cook and his wife, Belle, to the Santa Ana Valley in 1874 is lost in the mists of time. What is certain is that when he left about a half dozen short years later, there was a crossroads village, a school district and a church—all the yeast and flour of the community that would eventually become a suburban metropolis.

It's easy to think of Orange County's boom as having taken place in the late 1940s and 1950s. In truth, the area has long had a series of boom-and-bust cycles. This was just the first. In fact, it wasn't even an Orange County boom—the partition of this region from Los Angeles County didn't take place until 1889.

In 1874, Cook came into possession of a 160-acre (later 200-acre) plot of land in the future Garden Grove. Today, the boundaries would be roughly Lampson Avenue and Garden Grove Boulevard north and south, with Euclid (now Main) Street and Nutwood Street east and west. The land had been purchased by C.E. Palmer, who sold it to Cook for the sum of $2,280. Soon buildings began to rise, although the location of the Cook home is subject to dispute.

According to *The History of Garden Grove*, written by H.C. Head and published in 1939, Cook lived in a brightly painted two-story wooden frame building a short distance west of what is now Main Street. But in *The Village of Garden*

Grove, author Leroy Doig places Cook in a one-story "California" house at the southeast corner of Nelson Street and Lampson Avenue. Presumably, a man of many vocations and talents had more than one address.

Readers interested in researching the history of the community will receive an interesting lesson on local geography. Garden Grove Boulevard, for instance, has been variously known as the Westminster Road and Ocean Boulevard. Euclid was once called the Anaheim Road, not to be confused with Anaheim Boulevard.

If the names of the roadways offer an interesting study in ambiguity, the naming of the community also allows considerable room for speculation. Mrs. J.D. Price, one of the community's pioneers, said that Cook named the newly planted school district Garden Grove, which applied itself to the village as well. In subsequent years, the story has arisen that some early settlers expressed skepticism about using such a grandiose name for the flat, featureless and largely uncultivated plains that spread out in every direction.

The story has Cook replying, "Then we'll make it appropriate by planting trees and gardens." And Garden Grove did soon become a garden and a grove, serving as an agricultural center for the next eighty years or so. Even the suburban sprawl that displaced the orange trees has a verdant look to it. Drive along Lampson Avenue (especially between Brookhurst and Magnolia Streets, for example) and you'll find yourself traveling under a leafy canopy of many varieties of lush, mature trees. Cruise along the Garden Grove Freeway as it rises above the tree line, and it looks like someone scattered a bunch of cars, houses and streets in the midst of an evergreen forest.

No surviving records offer more than just hints to Cook's inspiration about the name. One clue may be offered by the small town of Garden Grove, Iowa, however.

In April 1846, a group of Mormon pioneers led by Brigham Young were continuing on their long trek westward toward the new Zion of Utah, fleeing from the prosecution and violence that had taken the life of the church's founder, Joseph Smith. In the south central part of the Hawkeye State, they founded a semi-permanent camp for traveling members of the Church of Jesus Christ, Latter-Day Saints.

Some members of the party stayed to establish the camp, planting gardens (hence the name) for food for themselves and those who would follow. The area became known as the "Mormon Trail," the name that has been adopted by the local school district there.

Eventually, the town emptied of Mormons, and people of other faiths settled in Garden Grove, Iowa. The town boomed in the early part of the twentieth century, becoming home to a thriving business district, several factories and a college. But in recent years, the population has declined, businesses have fled and now the number of residents has dropped to below three hundred people, "about half of them senior citizens," according to the city clerk.

Did Cook know of the original Garden Grove, and was he inspired by the name? Many Mormons lived in the area at the time and might have suggested it. The plain truth is that we don't know. But the Mormon legacy lives on here. The LDS Church has long had a strong presence in this Garden Grove; indeed, for a time, the area around Buaro Street north of Garden Grove Boulevard was once popularly known as "Mormonville." More recently, Bruce Broadwater, a member of the LDS Church, was the city's longest-serving mayor.

Whatever the inspiration for the name, it stuck. Cook helped establish many of the institutions of the early community, luring businesses, residents and churches to the town. Even if Cook did not stay around for very long, it's still fair to say that without him, there might not have been a distinct "place" here, under whatever name.

Cook helped stock his new village with friends and relatives. His father-in-law, David Webster, came to town to become its first postmaster (the post

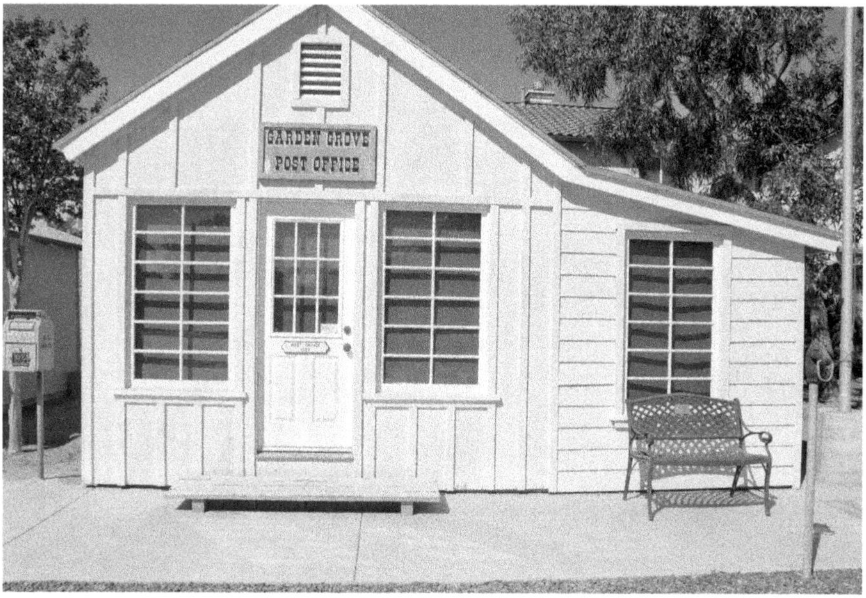

Garden Grove's original post office, dating back to the 1870s, is preserved at the Stanley Ranch. *Author's collection.*

office being established in 1876–77) and a pillar of the community. Webster was active in the founding and growth of the First Methodist Church—Garden Grove's earliest house of worship—and was popularly known as "Deacon Webster." While the church was established in 1875 under a Methodist charter, it was really open to Protestants of all denominations.

The deacon came to the Santa Ana Valley by a circuitous route. Born in England in 1815, he was a founder of the forerunner of the Young Men's Christian Association. He was sixty-one when he came to Garden Grove and later was justice of the peace in nearby Westminster.

Garden Grove's first merchant was Converse Howe, who was also lured by Cook and who started up the Howe & Co. store (Cook held a half-interest) in 1877. The first blacksmith was George Little, who set up shop in 1876.

Cook helped spur development by subdividing his property and selling off lots to the pioneering families of the new community. With a church, school, post office, blacksmith shop and general store, the seeds were planted for the establishment of a village. By 1880 or 1881, when Cook is believed to have left Garden Grove, the new settlement was well on its way to permanence and progress.

Chapter 3

IT TAKES A VILLAGE

Americans—especially Californians—have never been very much in awe of history. That's one of the reasons we tend to demolish old buildings without much regret. Our culture looks forward, not backward, which is part of our unique and dynamic national character.

It's not an unalloyed virtue, however. There's a lot to be learned from the past, especially from your own past. We can discover much about how our lives and worlds came to be as they are by taking a thoughtful look at the evidence of things departed.

If you're looking for places and settings to conjure up the memory of Garden Grove's village era (roughly from its founding to the coming of the railroad in 1905), you won't find very much that survived the ravages of time, street widening and the voracious escrow.

A visit to the Garden Grove Historical Society's Stanley Ranch Museum and Historic Village (a short distance south of Chapman Avenue) is the best place to re-create history, although most of the restored (or recreated) buildings are from the town period (1905–41). To truly understand Garden Grove's salad days, you need not a street map but a vivid imagination.

The first thing to remember is that the Garden Grove of this time—indeed, up until the postwar boom—was just a small fraction of the municipality that we identify as the City of Youth and Ambition. Instead of sprawling across eighteen square miles and stretching from horizon to horizon along the busy freeway, this village was just a few hundred yards square. Travel north to where Chapman Avenue is and you begin to enter a terra incognita of farmland and trees. Garden Grove in this time was about a half mile in each direction from its epicenter at what is now Main Street and Garden Grove Boulevard. The village would creep slowly outward from that location, its evident borders presaged somewhat by the much larger Garden Grove (Elementary) School District (GGSD) and enlarged by the boom of the mid-twentieth century to a degree that the founding fathers might have found fantastic.

In fact, the founding and early years of the public school district—along with the farming industry and the churches—mirrors the growing pains of the little village. The GGSD, forerunner to the huge Garden Grove Unified School District, the third-largest in Orange County, was officially established in the fall of 1874. The previously unnamed area had been under the jurisdiction of the old Bolsa Grande School District, whose name survives as the GGUSD's third high school, opened in 1959.

The first classes were taught by Mrs. Alice L. Armor in the small wooden house of the Methodist minister. In the fall of 1875, a more permanent home was established, a one-room schoolhouse on the site of what is now Zlaket's Market. The building cost $800, and Miss Belle Squires presided over a student body of twenty-five.

Two years later, for reasons unknown, people in the northwest area of the district split off and formed a new public school entity, the Alamitos School District, headquartered where Marie Hare Continuation High School is now located. It would be a separate school system until the GGSD, ASD and Garden Grove Union High School District were unified in 1965.

Enrollment rose and fell with the economic fortunes of the time. When a new two-story Garden Grove Public School was built in 1884 near the old school, there were now two teachers with a student body that rose slowly to a peak of 187 by 1894, when a faculty of four teachers was on hand.

The old Public School—also variously known as the Grammar School, Village School and Euclid School—has a certain Tom Sawyeresque feel to it. Go to Kaye's Kitchen on Main Street and find a photo of the school and students from that era and see many a bare foot and lopsided grin looking at you from another century. Horses and bicycles were the means of transport, and corporal punishment and ridicule were liberally employed to keep miscreants in line.

"In the corner, on a stool, reposed the dunce camp," remembered Horace Head. "It was about two feet high. Unless you have endured this type of punishment, augmented by the laughter of your classmates, you have never known the ultimate in humiliation."

It wasn't the only school in the area. Near the intersection of what is now Westminster Avenue and Harbor Boulevard, at what was then the southeastern limit of the GGSD, there was a "squatter" community of people who claimed the land was government property and open to free use. To educate their children, the district sent a teacher to establish the Willow School, so named because of the willows, cottonwoods and sycamore trees in the marshy area. After four years, the Willow experiment ended, and pupils had to travel to Garden Grove proper to get their dose of book-learning.

There was also a "Mormon school" at Buaro Street and Garden Grove Boulevard for a time, as well as a school in the Newhope district in the southern part of the old GGSD, in an area that is now part of Santa Ana. Additionally, a Seventh-Day Adventist Church school was established in 1897.

The early local schools only went up to the eighth grade; students wishing to pursue the then-lofty goal of a high school diploma attended one of the "nearby" high schools in Santa Ana, Orange or Anaheim. It wasn't until 1921 that Garden Grove High School first opened its doors.

The other communal experience for early Grovers was to be found in the church. It's been said that the present-day city has more churches per capita than any other community in Orange County, and looking back at its history, it's not hard to see why. Churches took root and grew faster than just about any crop, and no fewer than four are still functioning into their third century of activity.

The oldest religious community in Garden Grove is what is now the United Methodist Church, situated on a modern campus at the southwest corner of Stanford Avenue and Main Street. It has gone through four sanctuaries and traces its origins to the very first days of the village.

The earliest antecedents go to 1874, when Sunday school classes were held in a room in Dr. Cook's home. In November 1875, the church was organized, with services being held in a schoolhouse. In 1878, the growing congregation was ready to commit to building its own church edifice, and construction was finally completed in 1879.

By 1884, the 112-member congregation was sufficient to warrant a full-time minister, Reverend R.A. Henry. A parsonage was added, and a temperance group sprung from the church's membership.

In 1891, the Alamitos Friends Church was established with thirty-nine charter members near the present site at Magnolia Street and Chapman Avenue. Now called the Garden Grove Friends Church, it is the oldest active "Quaker" congregation in Orange County.

The Seventh Day Adventist Church was born in 1895, and the First Baptist Church was first convened in 1897. One local church that did not survive was one affiliated with a "breakaway" group called the Reorganized Church of Jesus Christ, Latter-Day Saints, that did not recognize the leadership of Brigham Young.

In keeping with the name of the new community, almost everyone in town farmed or in some way owed their living to agriculture. Garden Grove, in its pre-urban days, went through many phases of specialization. The middle-aged resident of today can remember the strawberry fields and orange groves of youthful days, but those crops are relative newcomers.

At first, farmers grew corn on the wide, flat spaces of Garden Grove land. The plentiful artesian wells that drew from the high water table below the surface were sufficient for a small family farm. Later, the coming of more residents and gasoline-powered pumps to provide more irrigation helped prompt a diversification into raising livestock, poultry, eggs and, eventually, fruits and nuts.

Raisins were a major crop for a while, until a vine disease, followed by a soaking rain, wiped out that industry locally. The grapes for raisins gave way to rows of walnut trees, and by 1890, the first orange trees were established. They would eventually become the dominant agricultural product of Garden Grove, but not before chili peppers, eucalyptus oil and a few others had their days.

The schools, churches and farms of the era were held to modest dimensions by the issue of transportation. Roads were few and universally unpaved; some were mere cow paths that turned to sticky muck under the rain. The automobile was still a creature of the next century. The vehicle of dreams for Garden Grove and all of Santa Ana Valley was the locomotive.

The Southern Pacific (SP) Railroad, created in 1870, was the entity that brought reliable, cheap transportation—as well as growth—to what were then the "outlying" areas of Southern California. The SP publicized the paradise of sunny SoCal across the nation, leading an influx of hopeful new residents to the Los Angeles area. The railroad pushed its lines toward the edges of the populated counties, with the SP reaching Anaheim in 1875. The arrival of the railroad spurred the growth of the Santa Ana Valley and gave a hint of what the iron horse could do for—and to—a community.

Henry Huntington's Pacific Electric system—soon to be famous for the "Red Car" line—began to snake its way out from central L.A. in the late 1880s. By 1905, it had reached Garden Grove, slicing diagonally through the community and bringing the village into the closer embrace of the world outside.

Garden Grove's downtown before the coming of the automobile. *Garden Grove Historical Society.*

With a railroad depot, the crossroads changed almost overnight into a burgeoning town, as farmers and growers took advantage of the shipping facilities offered. Packing houses grew up nearby, and a general increase in population and economic activity was reflected in the expansion of the once-tiny business district. Banks, newspapers, retail operations of all kinds, new subdivisions and more appeared quickly, fertilized by the promise offered by a convenient connection with customers and suppliers from beyond the meadow. The second phase of the community's life was about to begin.

Chapter 4

OUR TOWN

The Greeks look back on the days of Pericles and Marathon as their golden age: some Americans look at our current crop of leaders and long for the days of Washington, Adams and Jefferson. If a community can be said to have a golden age, then perhaps for Garden Grove it was the time from the coming of the railroad to the bombing of Pearl Harbor.

During that period, Garden Grove developed into a full-fledged town complete with a fire department, high school, street lights, busy downtown, commuter rail service to all points north and south and a hardworking but slow-paced small-town lifestyle that sounds pretty appealing to many of us caught up in the hectic, stressful pressures of twenty-first-century life. Voluntary cooperation would solve many problems then in a way that might seem unlikely today.

Of course, memories can be selective. Garden Grove was not in all ways a bucolic paradise. When it rained, it flooded. Paved streets and lighting were by no means universal, and racial and ethnic prejudices were often not far below the surface. A devastating earthquake would level much of the central business district. Residents of the community would turn their backs on cityhood, and there being no local government (until 1956), many of the problems that still plague Garden Grove today were planted in this laissez faire era when people—good and bad—were pretty much left alone to fend for themselves, which resulted in both prodigies of creativity and stupidity.

In 1910, just a few years after the Pacific Electric brought regular passenger and freight service to town, the population was put at about 1,200, triple what it had been in 1890. In 1940, just before the end of the era, the figure had risen to about 5,500, but even that number was just a hint of the possibilities to beckon after the world came back from war.

The biggest catalyst for the town era was the railroad: the Pacific Electric (PE) railway. Henry Huntington in 1903 decided to extend the PE south and east to Santa Ana, and a diagonal route was chosen that cut across Buena Park, Stanton and Garden Grove. Construction started on October 1, 1904, and through service to Santa Ana began on November 6, 1905.

Garden Grove's depot was located west of Euclid (now Main) Street and north of Garden Grove Boulevard. Ironically, the Home Depot parking lot is now the site of the former rail depot. The angle at which the railway right of way ran created some odd-shaped parcels and cut chunks of land and city blocks in half.

Instantly, the railroad worked a major change in the community. It provided not just passenger but also shipping service. An industrial park of sorts sprang up around the depot, led by large orange-packing facilities. These buildings went through many incarnations—packinghouse, thrift store, mattress outlet, etc.—before finally being leveled in the late 1980s.

The railway made Garden Grove into a significant shipping point for farmers and growers in the surrounding area, which in turn spurred the growth of businesses in the small community. The downtown of old, which had been a somewhat scraggly accumulation of wooden and stone structures,

Downtown Garden Grove as it appeared in 1909. *Garden Grove Historical Society.*

Garden Grove's citrus produce was marketed under a variety of brands. *Author's collection.*

blossomed into a brick-and-mortar center of greater permanence. Many of the leading institutions of the community—chamber of commerce, newspaper, etc.—date from this time and this rail-fired boom.

Best known to contemporary residents is the old "Red Car" interurban railways of legend. The Red Car connected Garden Grove with locations all across Orange and Los Angeles Counties, making trips to Newport or Pasadena (in the era before wide, paved roads) relatively easy, quick and convenient.

The rail not only made it possible for Garden Grove to export its products and provide new opportunities for its residents, but it also brought the world here. Midwestern families seeking to come to the milder climate of California were part of the "boxcar culture" that fueled the community's modest but steady growth. Families, or groups of families, would rent boxcars in Iowa or Michigan and fill them with animals, furniture, kith and kin and make the long, aromatic but inexpensive trip across the plains, up and over the big divide to finally arrive at this bustling little town. Early Garden Grovers would gather at the depot to see what new family was arriving; some friendships,

The Pacific Electric depot in 1921, twelve years after the railroad came to town. *Garden Grove Historical Society.*

business relationships and perhaps even romances were kindled that first day on the rough wooden steps of that depot.

The original electric line gave way to diesel engines, and after the demise of the Red Car line in the late 1940s, freight service became the main purpose of the line. Baby boomers who grew up in Garden Grove can easily recall the long, slow progress of the trains through the summer days, the motormen returning the excited waves of kids, who always seem to be fascinated by trains.

(Garden Grove is still served by rail. A Union Pacific freight line runs north–south through West Garden Grove's central industrial district, connecting at its head with another line that runs east–west from Disneyland to Cypress.)

Some of the nostalgia for the old Red Cars that in part fuels the support for various rail proposals today is genuine, while some employs selective memory or mythology. It is true that carmakers, bus lines and tire manufacturers benefited from the demise of the old interurban lines, but the growth in auto traffic had already led to a decline in the usage of the Red Line. As more people owned their own cars, fewer used the trolley, and more cars meant crowded streets, which slowed the movement of the rail cars (which ran at grade, crossing many streets in the process) to a crawl, which in turn discouraged many riders from using the system.

Top: A museum re-creation of a section of the Pacific Electric railway that cut through Garden Grove. *Author's collection.*

Bottom: The Red Car trolley line linked Los Angeles to Orange County and ran through Garden Grove. A new streetcar system for Santa Ana and Garden Grove is being contemplated at this writing. *Orange County Archives.*

But all that was still years away when the iron horse came to Garden Grove and worked its transforming magic. The boom was on, and the community began to spread out. The "central business district" of the community reached from just south of Euclid (Main) north to Stanford Avenue, then west and east of Euclid to Verano (now the realigned "southern leg" of Euclid).

Residential tracts were established that extended the community north to Lampson Avenue and in the southwesterly direction to Brookhurst Street and Trask Avenue by 1930.

Having their birth in this era were the Garden Grove Chamber of Commerce (originally the Garden Grove Improvement Association) in 1907, the *Garden Grove News* newspaper (1909), the first public street lighting (1911, along what's now Main Street) and the first paved roads (1912, again on Main Street).

Two catastrophes of a very different nature hit the community in the early town era. In February 1916, heavy rainfall resulted in an overflow of the Santa Ana River, which poured across the central part of Orange County. The raised bed of the PE served as an unintentional levee, meaning that land east and north of the railroad was flooded several feet deep, while those south were relatively unscathed. One man, J.K. Beardsmore, drowned in a channel of floodwaters near Harbor Boulevard.

Finally, the railroad embankment was dynamited in four places by "persons unknown," dropping the water level in most of old Garden Grove

When the Santa Ana River overflowed in 1916, much of Garden Grove was underwater. *Garden Grove Historical Society.*

to a tolerable height. Later that year—as part of a general cleanup and in preparation for future downpours—the railway was lowered from a height of three and a half feet to grade level within a half mile of the depot.

The greater catastrophe of the time was World War I, which resulted in a boom of sorts locally. After the Armistice in 1918, Garden Grove experienced a modest increase in developing of homes. Property values increased sharply, and the town spread south and west.

By the 1920s, the town had grown up enough to take up two issues central to any burgeoning community: schools and government. Since the founding of Garden Grove, youngsters wishing to attend high school had traveled to Anaheim or Santa Ana for that purpose. But in 1919, a new state law made it possible for high school districts to annex neighboring school districts if they served as the high school of choice. Thus, Santa Ana moved to gobble up the Garden Grove and Tustin school systems, a state of affairs that riled local pride and led to the establishment of the Garden Grove Union High School District (GGUHSD) in March 1921. The new GGUHSD (whose area embraced the elementary district boundaries of the Garden Grove, Alamitos and Bolsa Grande systems) opened its doors in temporary quarters with sixty-three students that September.

In 1922, the school moved to its present site on Stanford Avenue. In 1923, the main classroom building was finished, a two-story structure. Only the foundation survived the 1933 Long Beach Earthquake.

In its early years, the school's athletic teams bore the nickname of the "Chili Peppers," after the leading agricultural product of the community at the time. By the late 1920s, though, the more dignified term "Argonauts" had been adopted. "Grove," as it is commonly called today, continues as one of the oldest high schools in Orange County (only Anaheim, Santa Ana, Huntington Beach, Fullerton and Orange are older), with over fifty-five thousand alumni who include celebrities and common folks alike.

The postwar boom also fired enthusiasm for the creation of a city government. Back in the 1920s, incorporated cities were more the exception than the rule, but some residents could see the benefits of having control over their own laws, public safety, streets, etc. Several attempts were made to make Garden Grove a city, but all failed. An effort in 1916 foundered on the issue of the boundaries of the proposed municipality. In 1922, the matter made it all the way to the ballot, but farmers worried about "higher city taxes" helped defeat the proposal by a vote of 227–186.

Another effort was made in 1930, but again voters turned thumbs down, voting to reject by a count of 359–262. It would take two more tries (one it 1955 and one in 1956) before local citizens would finally agree to create a city.

Some observers trace Garden Grove's problems to the absence of a municipal government for the first three-quarters of a century of its existence, and there is certainly some truth to this. County government—especially in that time—provided little in the way of services to unincorporated towns and practically nothing in terms of planning and development.

As a result, areas of the town that would eventually become Garden Grove include some hodge-podge construction, rundown buildings and generally chaotic land use. Some of the older sections of Garden Grove Boulevard are a testimony to the county's leadership—or the lack of it—in the pre-incorporation era.

On the other hand, not all of the blame can be placed in Santa Ana, the county seat. Even in those days, city governments were limited in their activities, and the sort of micro-managed community development that's common today—even specifying the sort of plants to be used in landscaping and dictating the color scheme of buildings—was unheard of during this

Garden Grove firefighters in a practice drill. *Author's collection.*

era. Having a City of Garden Grove a generation or two earlier might have had some significant positive effects, but the absence of a local city hall is probably not to blame for the fact that we don't live in paradise.

Even though there was no official city, Garden Grove did enjoy some benefits of urban life. In the 1920s, two local water companies were organized to supply running water to homes in town, and in 1924, the Garden Grove Sanitary District was formed by a 219–38 vote, creating a sewer system.

A series of fires led to the creation of a Garden Grove Volunteer Fire Department, and in 1927, voters approved the creation of the Garden Grove Fire Protection District, which was the forerunner of the Garden Grove Fire Department.

The 1930s would bring more upheaval, both from Mother Earth and Wall Street. First, the stock market crash and the Great Depression that followed would bring the world's economic system to its knees, and then the Long Beach Earthquake would level much of the town of Garden Grove.

Chapter 5

COLLAPSE

When the earth shook and the walls came down in 1933, it might have seemed to the town's residents that it was just Mother Nature imitating the upheaval the mortal economic universe was still experiencing.

On March 10 of that year, just like the rest of the nation, Garden Grove was waiting to see if the new president inaugurated a few days prior—Franklin D. Roosevelt—could do something to alleviate the crushing financial depression that began with the 1929 stock market crash and that by '33 had reached into every corner of the world.

"I was thirteen," recalled Donita Jordan Reynolds. "Our English Club was having a pot luck in the [Garden Grove Union High School] cafeteria. Several of us had come early.

"All of a sudden, it began shaking and we all started to run. Things fell out of the lockers. We ran outside. Something falling from the building hit the back of my head. I still have the scar," said Reynolds.

"Falling debris killed Elizabeth Pollard four feet from where I'd fallen. Another girl was also hit. As I lay on the steps, something told me I was going to die. I thought, 'No, I'm going to get out of here.' I went down the steps to the lawn and passed out."

The quake—which was actually centered closer to Huntington Beach than Long Beach—tore through the reinforced masonry that comprised much of the old town. The second floor of the high school's main building was a total loss, and the structure would eventually have to be torn down to the foundation. Virtually all of the business district was

Garden Grove News

QUAKE ROCKS MANY SECTIONS

Huge Property Damage Here As Result of Quake

Practically Every Building In Business District Damaged---Many Are Completely Demolished

ELECT TRUSTEES FOR SANITARY DISTRICT

PLANS OUTLINED FOR REBUILDING STRICKEN AREA

Local Bank Gets Opening Order

MERRY SCHOOL PARTY TURNED INTO TRAGEDY

GARDEN GROVE EMBRACES OUT DOOR LIFE

Following In the Wake of the Quake

CURES EFFECTED BY QUAKE

Garden Grove News, established in 1909, chronicled the 1933 earthquake. *Garden Grove Historical Society.*

The 1933 Long Beach Earthquake drove some merchants to sell their goods in the middle of Euclid Street. *Garden Grove Historical Society.*

damaged, although some structures collapsed entirely, while others came through with lesser damage.

"The two houses in town that completely went down were stone houses, and one was ours," remembered Anna Mae Devine Newman. The quake struck at 5:55 p.m., just before dinner was to be served.

"We had a rule we ate dinner at six. Dinner was ready, but I was with my mother and brother Ray in our yard near our chickens and rabbits. The earth moved and everybody was yelling and not knowing what was going on. A chimney next door fell down. Our brick house collapsed."

The quake knocked out electricity, gas and even water in some locations. Many residents, fearing aftershocks, slept outside or in cars even if their homes were undamaged.

After the earth stopped shaking, local townspeople went into action to help the needy and protect the vulnerable. The fire department turned out quickly, but luckily there were no fires. With no local police department, guard duty around collapsed buildings was provided by the local chapter of the American Legion, the organization formed for World War I veterans.

The falling down of shops and homes coincided with the dawn of the New Deal, which aimed to raise up the deflated economy. FDR opened his new administration with a flurry of action, including the bank holiday that stopped the runs on savings institutions and began to bring the banking industry under the control of Uncle Sam. The same American Legionnaires who kept curiosity-seekers out of unsafe buildings also helped enforce the bank holiday.

The Great Depression was the longest and most severe economic downturn in American history. At its peak—or nadir—one out of four American workers was unemployed, a situation made worse by the absence of unemployment insurance, the one-earner family and the evaporation of billions of dollars of savings into failed banks.

"Everyone was struggling during the Depression," said Roy Littlejohn, who grew up in Garden Grove during those dark days. "But when you're tossed in the water, you learn to dog paddle."

Local charity included bread lines, but that only went so far in an era before food stamps and welfare. Handouts still had the aroma of laziness.

"Most everybody worked back then," said Littlejohn. "No matter what it was, even selling pencils. Kids worked, and things were tough."

"We never felt poor," recalled Carol Schnitger, who grew up on Garden Grove Boulevard in a house now being used as a glass and mirror store. "But tramps, 'gentlemen of the road,' would often come by and ask my mother

Citrus growing, packing and shipping was big business in Garden Grove. The Mutual packinghouse was one of the largest in the area. *Garden Grove Historical Society.*

for food as they walked down the Red Car tracks. They camped out in the tracks near the Santa Ana River. They'd make a little fire and eat dinner out of a tin can."

The ethos of the time was to make do with what was available. "We grew everything we ate," said Jim Gupthill, who lived on a farm near Magnolia Street. "We didn't have any money. It wasn't all that bad; we just lived different. Once in a while my dad would take five bucks and go down to buy essential things in the grocery store. I had one pair of shoes back then. Instead of buying me a new pair of shoes, he bought me rubber glue-on soles. Maybe they'd stick on my old soles, maybe not."

Even though the Depression was a powerful setback to the economic fortunes of the community, it was not as profound a catastrophe as in more urbanized areas. Farmers always have food. And the community still found the money to pay for things it felt it needed.

In the wake of the '33 quake, Garden Grove was given an unexpected chance to start over. Some of the larger businesses, such as the Mutual Orange Distributors, began rebuilding almost immediately, although this time with steel-reinforced concrete.

A group of business and community leaders assembled into the Euclid Improvement Association, a private forerunner of the public redevelopment agencies that existed from the 1970s through 2012. The EIA came up with a plan that called for the widening of Euclid (now Main) Street to a new width of seventy-two feet, with a Spanish Mission style of architecture featuring white walls and red tile roofs. Many of the older surviving buildings on Main Street retain elements of the urban design fashions of the 1930s.

In addition to rebuilding the downtown, Garden Grove's high school needed considerable attention, and not just because of the earthquake. The economic collapse led to a sudden slide in tax revenue, creating a deficit for the GGUHSD. The earthquake demanded repairs at the high school, and voters swept both problems aside with a bond election paired with a tax override.

The main building at the school had to be replaced. With help from FDR's Works Projects Administration (which also built a second classroom building), the old structure was torn down to the foundation, on which a new one-story replacement was built. That's now known as Heritage Hall, as it hosts an extensive display of school history, in addition to classrooms and offices.

Garden Grovers proved they could take a punch and roll with it. But a greater storm was brewing across two oceans that would reach into this small but growing town.

Chapter 6

WINDS OF WAR

When World War II finally gathered America in its lethal embrace, the effects resounded far from the battlefield. Not only did Garden Grove give hundreds of its sons and daughters (of whom thirteen were killed) to the war against fascism, but it would also ultimately give up its way of life.

The war itself had relatively little impact on the town, but the changes it would usher in transformed everything. The peacetime boom that followed would far surpass any previous period of growth and would take a small agricultural town and make it into a large suburban city.

Huge groves of citrus trees that extended as far as the eye could see would soon become just a memory. The slow, personal pace and feel of the place would become quicker and more fluid; indeed, the community itself would expand far beyond what people meant when they thought of "Garden Grove." Institutions and people would come here who were once considered as exotic as spaceships and Martians.

Just seven hours after news first reached the West Coast that the Japanese had attacked Pearl Harbor on December 7, 1941, the townspeople had organized a watch for enemy aircraft.

"They used to have a guard watching for planes," recalled Clyde Gedney, who stood watch for Mitsubishi Zeros two hours a week. "They'd set you in a shack way out in the sticks, and you had to call in any airplane you saw."

Men watched during the night and women by day. Carol Schnitger shared lookout duty with her mother in a tiny building. "There was a large poster in there with the shapes and identifications of planes," she said. One airwatch station was located south of Garden Grove High, with another on Trask Avenue between Brookhurst Street and Magnolia Street, where—perhaps ironically—several Japanese car dealerships now help anchor the successful Garden Grove Auto Center.

The town had forty-nine blackout wardens, and the community was sometimes ordered to go dark. From the distance of time that separates us from the early days of American participation in World War II, the precautions taken by civil defense officials may seem excessive, even ludicrous. But in the excitement (some might say hysteria) of the time, they seemed prudent.

It's important to remember that with the decimation of the U.S. Pacific Fleet in Hawaii, little stood between the Imperial Japanese navy and the West Coast. While an invasion of California was always unlikely, the possibility of bombing attacks or even commando raids could not be ruled out. A Japanese submarine surfaced and shelled an oil field in Santa Barbara in February 1942, following closely on the "ghost" air raid over Los Angeles in December 1941 that was chronicled humorously in the Steven Spielberg film *1941*, starring John Belushi.

If the typical Garden Grove resident had little to fear from the war on the home front, some did suffer considerably. The community—indeed, much of West Orange County—was home to many Japanese residents, including hundreds of native-born U.S. citizens of Nipponese descent.

The press and the military did much to raise public anxiety about the Japanese in California. Immigrants living in Hawaii were accused of providing detailed information about American military dispositions in that territory, and the notion of a Pacific Coast honeycombed with Japanese espionage agents more loyal to Emperor Hirohito than President Roosevelt was encouraged by hysterical and sometimes racist accounts in newspapers and on the radio.

An executive order was soon issued from the federal government ordering the relocation and internment farther inland of Japanese nationals and even U.S.-born citizens from West Coast locations. Japanese living away from the coasts were not interned. Some Italians and Germans met a similar, if less publicized, fate.

"When the war began," recalled Jim Guptill, "they picked up the Japanese pretty quick." About one hundred Japanese and Japanese Americans lived in Garden Grove, supporting a private Japanese school and a Japanese mission at the First Baptist Church, and Tom and Mary Inouye ran a popular fruit stand in what is now the parking lot of the Costco warehouse store on Garden Grove Boulevard.

Outside of what was then considered Garden Grove proper, in the area known as Alamitos, many Japanese growers lived in what was called Chili Hot Town at the northwest corner of Magnolia Street and Garden Grove Boulevard, where a largely Asian shopping center now stands.

As the war wound down, Japanese internees were released from the camps in Arizona, New Mexico and Colorado, but few found their way back to Garden Grove and Orange County. Those who did have been reluctant to talk about the experience. It would be another two generations before a large Asian American population settled again in the community.

As the Japanese left, the military came to Garden Grove. An army detachment camped in the area now home to the ducks and geese in the ponds of the Civic Center Park behind the regional library at Euclid Street and Stanford Avenue. A prisoner-of-war camp for captured Germans was established on Garden Grove Boulevard, about a quarter mile west of Haster Street, across from the current site of Garden Grove Hospital and other buildings such as the Holiday Inn Express and senior citizen housing.

From 1944 to 1946, the camp corralled hundreds of captive "Krauts," many of whom were hired out to pick citrus fruit in the endless groves that occupied much of the land then. Many of the POWs preferred to pick oranges in the open air to being cooped up in camp.

There's a little more to the story. According to reports, a local woman developed a romantic attachment to one of the prisoners and helped him escape. She harbored him in her home in what now would be Anaheim until authorities tracked the fugitive down and returned him to the custody of Uncle Sam.

When the Germans were eventually repatriated after the war, the camp did not fall into disuse. For a while it was pressed into duty as housing for members of the bracero (manual labor) program, which provided guest workers from Mexico to come into the United States to be employed in the agriculture business. In Garden Grove, that would mostly have meant picking fruit. The bracero program was ended in 1964 amid complaints that the workers were exploited and unfairly competing with U.S. citizens for jobs.

One of the more short-lived but important military institutions in Garden Grove was Haster Air Field. Located in its heyday on a 160-acre plot between Trask Avenue on the north, Westminster Avenue to the north and Cannery Road (now Magnolia Street) to the west and extending to Wright Street (now Brookhurst Street), the one-time farm of Dick Haster was taken over by the U.S. Navy in 1944 as a primary flight training field for naval aviation cadets stationed at the new Los Alamitos Naval Air Station.

For three months, the Haster Air Field hummed with activity. "They'd have ten or fifteen planes for Los Alamitos that flew out of there," said Haster's son, also named Dick. "I remember there'd be a landing every five or six minutes. There was some night flying done there as well."

There was at least one crash and a few unauthorized touchdowns. But as quickly as the navy came, it disappeared. Haster didn't get his land back, though, because it was now surplus government property.

After eleven years of wrangling, Haster bought his land back at $2,600 an acre, compared to the $750 an acre he was paid by Uncle Sam back in 1944. An attempt to make a commercial airstrip of the site went for naught, and in the 1950s and '60s, the land was recycled into Bolsa Grande High School on the east and Garden Grove Park/Atlantis Play Center on the west.

More than Garden Grove's land went to war. Hundreds of locals fought in the great conflict. The Selective Service board was on Euclid (Main) across from Zlaket's Market in the chamber of commerce offices. The draft and patriotism had heavy impacts on not only the labor force but also on the student population.

Of the Garden Grove High School class of 1944, for instance, there were one hundred freshmen, but only fifty-seven graduated. "Many served in the war," said Schnitger. Her *Argonaut* yearbook listed 338 former Argos serving in the military.

Residents fought in every branch of the armed services, performing many heroic acts. One of the best remembered was Don Wakeham, a hero of the Battle of the Coral Sea. President of the class of 1937, Wakeham was the classic big man on campus, and for good reason. He was on the student council and student commission. He played football, basketball and tennis. He had his creative side, too—he was in the glee club and performed in four plays and an operetta.

"Oh, boy, do I remember Don," recalled Donita Jordan Reynolds. "He was a very handsome man and very popular with the girls...Don was a good high school student, a fine person and an excellent dancer."

Wakeham joined the U.S. Naval Reserve before World War II started and was sent to Pearl Harbor after the Japanese attack. A pilot, he was assigned to the aircraft carrier USS *Lexington*. He flew a type of plane that has since disappeared from the sky: the dive bomber.

In the days before missiles and laser-guided bombs, hitting a moving ship with a bomb was a very dicey proposition. So naval air forces developed the dive bomber, a carrier-based plane that would literally dive from a high

A Dauntless dive bomber of the type that Don Wakeham flew during the Battle of the Coral Sea. *Wikimedia Commons.*

The Japanese aircraft carrier *Shoho* sank during the Battle of the Coral Sea. *Wikimedia Commons.*

altitude almost vertically toward a target and release its lethal load as close as possible to the prey. The strain on man and machine was considerable, and casualties were high.

At the Battle of the Coral Sea, the first major action in the Pacific after Pearl Harbor, the U.S. and Japanese fleets fought to a bloody standoff. Now overshadowed by the bigger Battle of Midway, the Coral Sea battle (May 4–8) was significant in that it checked the progress of the Japanese advance and may have saved Australia from invasion.

Wakeham's squadron attacked the Japanese carrier *Shoho*, and he later described the action in this way: "We caught the ship flat-footed...We dived from about 18,000 feet to 2,500 and let the bomb go...I was lucky. I got my thousand-pounder right into her guts. It hit the carrier midships. A great yellowish flame, like a sunburst, was all I could see as I looked back."

Wakeham was awarded the Navy Cross for his accomplishment, but his career and life would be tragically short-lived. In November 1942, he failed to return from a second mission the same day fighting over the Solomon Islands. His plane attacked Japanese cruisers and the transport ships they escorted and helped shoot down two enemy aircraft, but he never made it back to base. He was awarded the Air Medal posthumously.

Chapter 7

PRIDE AND PREJUDICE

No event in Garden Grove since its founding had as profound an impact on the community as World War II. Aside from the personal sacrifices made by locals of all conditions and nationalities, the war set into motion a series of events that would forever change it, moving it into its third stage of development as a modern city.

How Garden Grove changed is in many ways an echo of how many rural towns became suburban giants in the postwar boom of babies and houses. The same forces that led to the subdivision of the old orange groves and strawberry fields into tract homes also created the shift from farm to city and city to suburb. There were, however, some impetuses unique to local circumstance that give this story its own special character.

The unseen cast in this tale of the community's new life includes Harry Truman, Walt Disney, Thurgood Marshall and Dr. Benjamin Spock. The avalanche of new ideas, new enthusiasms and new technology that the war began would soon bury the old, slow-paced life here and replace it with something quicker, flashier and certainly bigger.

A grateful nation, combined with practical politicians eyeing the impact of seventeen million veterans at the ballot box, rewarded the men and women in uniform with many benefits without precedent in America and, indeed, world history. The GI Bill (officially the Veterans Readjustment Act) and Veterans' Administration made it cheap and easy for vets to attend college, buy houses and move up into the middle class.

The pent-up demand for education, housing and marriage produced booms in the construction of colleges, homes, schools and babies.

California's key role in the defense industry of World War II had drawn many to the industrial plants and military bases of the West. Those visitors were so impressed by the balmy weather and wide-open spaces that they soon flocked to Southern California, one step behind the subdividers who began buying up agricultural property to build new suburbs.

Beginning in the late 1940s and continuing through the 1950s, America went from a nation of renters to a nation of homeowners and from a nation of people living on farms or in small towns to a nation of people living in big cities and the suburbs that surrounded them.

As the groves and farms began to disappear across Orange County, people began to pour in. In 1948, a special census by the State of California predicted that Garden Grove would reach the unheard-of population of 20,000 by 1970. While the figure suggested bigger things to come, it missed the mark by over 100,000 people.

Returning war vets were only part of the reason for the boom. The Santa Ana Freeway pushed south, and the state began to plan a whole network of freeways that would make living in the one-time hinterlands of San Fernando Valley and Orange County much more practical propositions. The arrival of the "5" freeway in Anaheim gave Walt Disney his best reason to locate his "Kiddie Land" project on Garden Grove's doorstep on cheap orchard land. The opening of Disneyland in 1955 gave a renewed boost to the county as a desirable place, and one success followed another.

Although fate and economics were pushing the community into its future, it still retained much of its past, some of it not worth hanging on to. Perhaps the most shameful heritage attached to Garden Grove was its segregation of Mexican children to a separate school after 1929. The local district was not alone in this; similar practices were followed in the Westminster, Santa Ana and El Modena school systems. The legal battle that followed would mean that the road to the triumph of the civil rights movement in America in the 1960s traveled through Orange County in the 1940s.

Most history books point out the significance of *Brown v. Board of Education*, a U.S. Supreme Court ruling in 1954 that declared that racial segregation in public schools was unconstitutional. But the lesser-known *Mendez v. Westminster* in many ways paved the way for that ruling. And, ironically, it was an act of racial discrimination against a different minority that helped make this pivotal lawsuit possible.

It all started in 1943 in an era when Orange County was an overwhelmingly white, famously conservative rural stronghold. Four local school districts—El

Sylvia Mendez, honored by President Barack Obama, was a plaintiff in the case that helped end racial segregation in California public schools. *Author's collection.*

Modena, Garden Grove, Santa Ana and Westminster—made a practice of segregating Mexican children into separate schools.

The Mendez family moved from Santa Ana to Westminster, leasing a rancho owned by a Japanese American family, who had been interned in Arizona as a consequence of war hysteria after Pearl Harbor. They were told that the Mendez children—sons Gonzalo Jr. and Jerome and daughter Sylvia—could not enroll in the nearby Seventeenth Street School (on present-day Westminster Boulevard) and instead had to attend the Hoover School, where the Mexican kids were sent.

Rebuffed by the Orange County Department of Education, parents Gonzalo and Felicitas hired a Los Angeles attorney to sue the Westminster School District in federal court. The class action lawsuit was enlarged to include all the local districts that practiced the segregation, and it was filed on March 2, 1945. Four other families joined the suit, which was supported by several civil rights groups, including the NAACP and the ACLU.

What followed was not the finest day for local public schools. The Garden Grove superintendent, for instance, testified in court that Mexican students needed separation from white kids because they were unable to compete academically with the lighter-skinned pupils.

At that time, the law of the land on segregation was still *Plessy v. Ferguson*, in which the Supreme Court in 1896 upheld the concept of "separate but equal" public schools. But the Mendezes' attorney argued that the facilities and supplies for Mexican kids were inferior and therefore not "equal."

On March 18, 1946, Judge Paul McCormick ruled for Mendez and the other plaintiffs. The local schools appealed the decision to the Ninth Circuit Court of Appeals in San Francisco, but the ruling was upheld.

As a consequence, Governor Earl Warren pushed the California legislature to also ban segregation of Asian and Native American children in schools. Warren would later become chief justice of the U.S. Supreme Court and presided over *Brown v. Board of Education.*

One of the "friend of the court" briefs in *Mendez v. Westminster* was written by the NAACP's Thurgood Marshall, who would also argue in the Brown case and was later appointed to the high court by President Lyndon Johnson.

In recent years, historians have begun focusing more attention on *Mendez* as an important precursor to *Brown* and the end of legal racial segregation in the United States. A postage stamp has been issued to commemorate the case, and an Emmy-winning TV documentary was filmed and has aired.

An elementary school in Santa Ana has been named after the Mendez family, and in 2011, Sylvia—that nine-year-old girl barred from the "white" school in 1943—was honored by President Barack Obama with the Presidential Medal of Freedom.

The Mendez case presaged Brown, which was a turning point in American history, jump-starting the civil rights movement, which would, in turn, inspire struggles for greater rights and opportunities for women, Hispanics, gays, the disabled and others.

Matters of race were a persistent undercurrent in all of Orange County. Some houses built in the early part of the boom were sold with codes, covenants and restrictions (CC&Rs) that would follow the house after it was sold. Today's CC&Rs are familiar to condo owners and usually deal with paint color and parking spaces, but back then some rules obligated new homeowners to agree not to sell their property to members of minority groups such as blacks, Jews, Mexicans and Asians. Those CC&Rs were struck down first by the courts and later by federal law, but they give us a hint as to what was on the minds of some of the developers who made Orange County into the large, populous region it is today.

Garden Grove grew. New tract communities sprang to life almost overnight. The commercial district snaked west and east along Garden Grove Boulevard. Garden Square was built in the early 1950s along the Boulevard west of Brookhurst Street and has been called Orange County's first shopping center. (Today, it is in the heart of the city's Korean business district, but most of the original buildings are still in use.)

Schools began to fill up in all three of the districts that served the community, and plans to add more took on urgency.

The old central business district around Main (Euclid) and the Boulevard still thrived, but competition from shopping areas "on the highway" began to chip away at its supremacy. The *Garden Grove News*, which had been a weekly newspaper since its inception in 1909, went to a twice-weekly schedule in 1952, reflecting both its growth and that of the community. The population

Garden Square on Garden Grove Boulevard is today called "Koreatown." *Garden Grove Historical Society.*

surged past the once-magic twenty-thousand figure and then leaped over the thirty-thousand number toward who-knew-where.

If you drive up Harbor Boulevard in Garden Grove, you'll see a skyline rising of hotels, with more on the way. It's the newly named Grove District of the Anaheim Resort area and is already bringing in thousands of tourists and millions of dollars in tax revenue to the city. But another venue of hospitality that preceded it has entered local history and folklore.

One legendary local institution that bloomed across this era was the Greenbrier Inn. The Inn and the associated Garden Grove Sanitarium hold a special place in not only the history of Orange County but in the heritage of the American film industry as well.

Located along Garden Grove Boulevard just west of Nutwood Street, those two establishments held more secrets and created more local folklore than any other place in the community.

The Sanitarium was opened in 1941 by Dr. Richard Carter, an Oxford grad with degrees in psychiatry and neurology. Along what was then a dusty two-lane road out in the sticks of Orange County, he built an "acute

Garden Grove Boulevard at Euclid Street in the mid-1950s. *Garden Grove Historical Society.*

psychiatric treatment center," which, in fact, turned out to be the Betty Ford Clinic of its day.

"They offered and produced secrecy there, and that's why it was successful," said local historian Marge Swenson. "Movie stars would disguise themselves in their butler's or maid's clothes and take the Pacific Electric Red Car down to Garden Grove."

Together with partner Roy Green, Carter operated the sanitarium for the glitterati of Hollywood and then toured Europe after World War II picking up expensive antiques at distress-sale prices. Back in Garden Grove, they opened the opulent Greenbrier just west of the hospital. Judy Garland was among the famous people who reportedly spent time detoxing there.

The Inn was the jewel of the city, even if its sylvan surroundings hid much of its light under a bushy bushel. The lobby and rooms were decorated with fourteenth-century suits of armor, Persian rugs, marble statues and more.

For decades, the Inn served multiple purposes. Friends and relatives of the rich and famous drying out at the sanitarium stayed and wined and dined at the Inn. Local functions were held there in a grand style, and many weddings, parties and even civic functions were celebrated in the hotel and adjoining cottages on the lushly landscaped grounds. The author's sister had her wedding reception at the Greenbrier in 1973.

That was near the end, though. Green, who ran the hotel, died "under mysterious circumstances" in Mexico several years later, and the Inn closed thereafter. The sanitarium held on for a few more years before it closed over licensing difficulties.

There are several eerie endings to the story. Carter was brutally slain by a houseboy who smashed a screwdriver through his skull. The accused claimed he acted in self-defense.

Dennis Witcher, a Garden Grove antiques dealer and history buff, told a spooky story about his efforts to appraise the value of items in the closed buildings: "Frankly, the place scared the hell out of me. There were marble-topped slabs that were used for postmortem examinations, rooms with dungeon-like cells…and rooms that looked like something right out of Frankenstein's windmill and I [saw all] of this by flashlight in a Gothic English setting."

But that's not how everybody remembers it. Judy Smith, who worked as a bookkeeper at the facility, has called some of the stories about the Inn and sanitarium "urban legends."

Even after closing, the complex had a second life as a clandestine destination for skateboarders who penetrated the grounds and used the empty swimming pool as a free skate park.

In the 1980s, a Newport Beach developer acquired the land and built a condominium complex and office building on the site. Other than the ceiling at the Azteca Mexican Restaurant on Main Street, formerly the bar at the Greenbrier, nothing remains of the place where Beverly Hills met Transylvania in the folklore of Orange County.

During much of the heyday of the Inn and Sanitarium, there was no official city here. Building and planning oversight (what there was of it) took place under the aegis of the County of Orange, which oversaw a dozen unincorporated towns rapidly mutating into young civic giants.

Costa Mesa incorporated as a city in 1953, as did Buena Park. After laying dormant for a quarter of a century, the notion of a City of Garden Grove awoke in 1955.

Chapter 8

THE BATTLE OF GARDEN GROVE

If you have a geographer's soul, you might have had some sport imagining what might have happened if there had never been a city of Garden Grove. A map published in a 1956 edition of the *Garden Grove News* showed the community truncated into the "Tail of Three Cities" as much of the area was stolen away by Anaheim, Orange and Santa Ana. It was those concerns and more that helped inspire the two epic political struggles that decided the community's fate in 1955 and 1956.

In fact, the story of incorporation intertwines significantly with the history of local journalism in Garden Grove. It might not be stretching the truth too much to say that enthusiastic—even somewhat slanted—coverage of the incorporation struggle tipped the scales in favor of creating a new city on the west county plains.

Newspapering in Garden Grove has a long and fairly vivid history. No fewer than seven newspapers have been published for the community, and an eighth was nearly started. Only two of them lasted for very long, and those two, the *Orange County* (originally *Garden Grove*) *News* and *Garden Grove Journal*, are still publishing and serving the community.

Although no copies are known to exist, some records refer to a *Garden Grove Artesian News* being briefly published in 1895. The first paper to take root was the *Garden Grove News*, a weekly founded in 1909 by U.S. Lemon of Anaheim, with its first issue on August 9 of that year.

The *News* changed hands several times in its first half century, changing formats, sizes and editorial policies. In 1955, though, the paper was purchased by the *Vancouver Sun*, which saw in the *News* a chance to get in on the ground floor of the tremendous expansion that was already transforming Orange County.

A new building, complete with offices, a pressroom, composing facilities and more, was constructed on Century Boulevard. The new owners began branching out the paper from Garden Grove, extending coverage and starting new papers and editions for nearby areas, reaching into Orange, Anaheim, Fullerton and Huntington Beach, as well as Westminster and Stanton.

At that time, the *Santa Ana Register* was the leading newspaper of Orange County, but more by default than any other cause. As the only daily with a countywide circulation, it was able to garner fifty thousand subscribers despite its low wages, ultraconservative editorial policies (which often spilled over into the news coverage) and a press plant that produced one of the inkiest and darkest papers around. (Since the 1980s, the *Register* has changed course and become an attractive, award-winning newspaper. It has won three Pulitzer Prizes and numerous other honors.)

Although Orange County has long been considered a conservative stronghold (only voting for a Democrat for president once, in 1936), that was changing by the mid-1950s. Many workers coming to O.C. from Los Angeles or even out of state were blue-collar people in highly unionized industries. That often meant a loyalty to the Democratic Party, and it seemed like the legions of new residents might prefer a paper more in line with their sympathies than the virulently anti-union, anti-government positions usually taken by the *Register*.

For the *Sun*'s plan to take hold, though, it needed a home base. That is, it needed a city in which to plant its flag and from which to carry its struggle. In 1955, that city seemed to be Garden Grove.

Incorporation, as we have seen earlier, had been tried before in Garden Grove, only to be rejected at the polls. But with the community rapidly growing every day and week, it seemed like the time was ripe to try again with a new group of voters.

Although this was no official city, residents did enjoy some local government, including three school districts, a fire protection district and a water and a sanitary district. Some people thought that was enough.

In 1950, Garden Grove's population was estimated to be 3,752. By the mid-1950s, it was approaching 40,000, and supporters of a new city won the right to put the issue on the ballot.

On March 10, 1955, voters spoke on cityhood for the first time in twenty-five years, but again the answer was "no." The tally was fairly close, but only 2,465 voted for incorporation, while 2,835 voted against.

This water tower in the downtown area was a local landmark until its demolition in 1969. *Garden Grove Historical Society.*

A scaled-down replica of the original Garden Grove fire station is located at the Stanley House Ranch Museum and Historical Village on Euclid Street. *Author's collection.*

"There was a big controversy over the expected rise in taxes by those who were against incorporation," said Harry Blades, one of the supporters of a new city and eventually one of its first city councilmen. "That's what beat us, because they convinced everybody taxes were going to go up. But the next time they cooled off quite a bit because they saw the handwriting on the wall."

The handwriting was annexation efforts by Anaheim and Orange. After the failure of Garden Grove cityhood in 1955, Anaheim sought to extend its boundaries well south of Katella Avenue, and Orange sought to move all the way west to Haster Street.

Defeat of the 1955 effort didn't daunt local incorporation supporters, who called for "home rule" and went to work right away. They hired a professional political consultant and got the not-inconsiderable support of the twice-weekly *News*. In those boom times, there were two other local papers, the *Rocket* and the *Pony Express*, but neither lasted long or had much influence.

The cityhood faction, led by Dean Eastman, got 2,390 signatures on a petition to call an election for April 17, 1956. The campaign that led up to the vote was enthusiastic and somewhat nasty.

At that time, Garden Grove was patrolled by county sheriff's deputies. Much was made of the fact that for all of the growing town, just one patrol car was assigned during the day and not even that at night. When calls for service came, cars often had to be summoned from other communities, sometimes at a considerable distance and delay.

The 1950s, with its booming numbers of children, was also a time of considerable concern over the issue of child molestation. Although we now know that many such crimes against youth are perpetrated by family members and other people known to the victim, back in 1956, the "friendly stranger in the black sedan" was thought to be the chief and likely culprit. In fact, the *News* even ran a full-page photo spread purporting to show how to avoid such predators, staging its scenes with the requisite man in the black Mercury offering candy out of the windows to clueless children.

It was significant because incidents of molestation were well publicized, and the *News* and other pro-cityhood forces sought to lead the public to the conclusion that the absence of a local police force increased the likelihood of your son or daughter being abducted or worse. To be against incorporation, the logic went, was to be on the side of the perverts.

The connection was not drawn just theoretically, as we'll see. In the thirteen months that had passed since the previous vote, Garden Grove's population had surged past forty-four thousand, and a largely new electorate turned in a new result: cityhood was a landslide winner this time, with 5,780 votes in favor and 2,346 against. Interested residents thronged the *News* office for the latest precinct tallies on the night of the election. In addition to voting for incorporation, the electors had also chosen the new municipality's first city council.

The Orange County Board of Supervisors certified the vote on June 15, and California secretary of state Frank Jordan declared Garden Grove to be the Golden State's newest city on June 18, the date that is usually observed as the city's birthday.

But the battle was not over, nor was the invective. Len Brown, leader of West Orange County Association Opposing Incorporation, sued in Superior Court to overturn the election. For two weeks, the issue of statehood hung in the legal balance.

The *News*, for its part, kept firing its ink ammunition. In each issue, it published an unflattering photo of Brown on the front page and called his group "S.M.O.G," which stood for "Selfish Minority of Gripers." Beneath the photo ran a tally of all the crimes—including molestations—that had occurred since election day, implying that Brown's opposition to cityhood was giving aid and comfort to criminals.

H. Louis Lake was Garden Grove's first mayor. *Garden Grove Historical Society.*

On July 2, the Orange County Superior Court rejected the challenge, and the Battle of Garden Grove was finally won. Although it wasn't the last shot fired in the conflict—the last appeal by opponents wasn't dismissed by a state court until December 8, 1958—it marked the beginning of the modern era in what would become the hometown for nearly 175,000 people.

H. Louis Lake, of the Lake family who owned and operated the Garden Grove Lumber and Cement Company, was chosen to be the city's first mayor.

The success of incorporation vindicated the *Sun*'s faith in Garden Grove, and right after the court ruling, the *Garden Grove News* became the *Daily News*, a six-day afternoon paper (no paper on Saturday; Sunday edition published in the morning) with an initial paid circulation of 11,500.

In many ways, the new *News* reflected the changes that West Orange County had gone through in just the past few years. It was the county's only union shop paper, compositors belonging to the International Typographical Union and reporters to the American Newspaper Guild. The publication endorsed Adlai Stevenson for president in 1956 and John Kennedy in 1960. And as Garden Grove and West Orange County grew, so did the *News*.

By 1964, it had become the *Orange County Evening News* and was owned by the national Ridder chain, which had plans to take on the *Register*. According to the story (never publically acknowledged but widely discussed), Ridder's plan was to also purchase the *Anaheim Bulletin*, *Newport News-Press* and *Costa Mesa Globe-Herald* and combine them with the *News* into a countywide publication based in Garden Grove.

Like so many grandiose plans (or legends), this one failed. The *Register* bought the *Bulletin*, the *Los Angeles Times* bought the Costa Mesa paper (which it renamed the *Orange Coast Daily Pilot*) and the Ridders seemed to lose enthusiasm for Orange County. Although the *News* continued to grow, reaching a peak of almost twenty-nine thousand paid circulation, it declined in the late 1960s because of competition from both the *Register* and the new (now-defunct) Orange County edition of the *Times*.

In August 1970, the *News* went to three times a week and later twice a week. In 1987, it was sold to local operators, and they in turn sold it in 1999 to Event Newspapers of Cypress, a firm that has now grown into Orange County Community Newspapers.

The new city was established as quickly as circumstances permitted. The old Fitz Intermediate School (originally Washington Grammar School) on Acacia Parkway, closed because of earthquake safety concerns, became the new city hall. A new age was most definitely underway.

Chapter 9

THE SILVER AGE

If the town era of the 1930s and '40s was Garden Grove's Golden Age, then perhaps one might label the late 1950s and '60s the Silver Age. Like the previous era, it was a precious time in which many of the institutions of the community were established and had their greatest influence.

During the period from 1956 to 1970, Garden Grove got its major shopping district, unified its three school systems into one, stretched itself west and east and rose to become the third-largest (now fifth-largest) city in Orange County. Garden Grove saw one of its own shot into space, saw another win Olympic glory and even incubated its own movie star, the comic actor and writer Steve Martin.

Municipally, Garden Grove's new city council moved quickly to not only establish a police force and absorb the existing Fire Protection District into a fire department but also to pull thousands of residents within city limits by annexing outlying areas. The original Garden Grove was a square city incorporating just the original town and recent subdivisions; before long, the new entity had extended fingers west and south to add new territory, growing from 11.5 square miles to 18.0 miles square miles today.

The most significant addition was the West Garden Grove area, which was once the eastern part of the Long Beach–based Bixby Ranch. Two developments, Eastgate and Garden Park, filled up much of the western wing of the city, joined to the rest of the community by a thin sliver of roadway along Garden Grove Boulevard. A large military installation that

Volunteer firefighters served the community from the 1920s until the city incorporated in the 1950s. *Garden Grove Historical Society.*

featured a Nike antimissile site comprised a third section, but that was declared surplus and developed as a light industrial manufacturing center east of Knott Street and west of the Union Pacific railway.

West Garden Grove emerged as the community's most affluent section, with many active youth sports groups. Pacifica High School, located at Lampson Avenue and Knott Street, serves as a sort of unofficial community center and common denominator for the westsiders. A bustling commercial strip running from the Garden Grove (22) Freeway north past Chapman Avenue along Valley View Street is the central business district for that portion of the city.

By 1960, the population of the growing city was 84,417, nearly double that of just four years before. It was touted as "America's Fastest-Growing City," and it was. Residents poured in at a rate of 46 a day, 1,428 a month.

In 1958, the city adopted its municipal seal, a green-and-orange design superimposed with a rendering of city hall with the slogan *Absit Invidia,* which means "without division or divisiveness." Later in 1960, in deference to the demographics of the community—46 percent of the population was under nineteen years of age—the city motto became "The City of Youth and Ambition."

Above: West Garden Grove is a distinct community within the city. The annual Little League/softball parade is a spring highlight. *Author's collection.*

Opposite, top: When houses replaced orange groves, packinghouses such as the Sunkist facility were sold and demolished. *Garden Grove Historical Society.*

Opposite, bottom: Garden Grove's citrus produce was marketed under a variety of brands. *Author's collection.*

A flood of new residents quickly wiped out most of the new city's agricultural past. Subdivisions conquered most of the once endless orange groves. The last major citrus grove in the community was leveled for a condominium complex in 1964. The old packinghouses were sold off or demolished, and now are all gone.

The city also moved to establish a park system. When Garden Grove incorporated, there was only the small Euclid Park downtown. The city acquired the old Haster Air Field site, with half going to the Garden Grove Union High School District as a site for Bolsa Grande High School and the other half to build Garden Grove Park, still the community's largest. At the north end is the gated Atlantis Play Center, a unique aquatic-themed recreation area.

One of the most enduring "modern" institutions dates from this era. The Strawberry Festival was born in 1959. With Sputnik overhead and Elvis on the transistor radio, the tradition of community celebration that started in

Sunkist
FOR SALE
GARDEN GROVE
CITRUS ASS'N.
Sunkist

GARDEN GROVE
PRIDE
VALENCIAS

Grovers Day was the precursor to the Strawberry Festival. In this photo, the Garden Grove High School band marches down Euclid (now Main) Street, circa 1955. *Garden Grove Historical Society.*

the 1930s with Grovers Day was refreshed with the new Strawberry Festival, celebrating what was then the community's leading crop.

The first festival was held on the west side of Brookhurst Way, north of the Boulevard. It featured a beauty pageant, a carnival midway, a "redhead roundup" and what was touted as the "world's largest strawberry shortcake" from Priscilla's Cakebox, then the community's premier bakery.

Francis X. Bushman, the silent film star, was the first celebrity grand marshal. The one-day event was such a success that the next year the festival was expanded to three days over Memorial Day weekend and moved to Garden Grove Park on Westminster Avenue.

There it stood until unruly crowds forced its move to the Village Green Park in the downtown area in 1973, where it's been ever since.

"It was a time when young people were rebelling against society," said Jan Dunn, who served as president of the Strawberry Festival Association the year it moved. "We moved the festival to its present location where it's near the police station and has better parking, and that seems to have taken care of the problem."

The Strawberry Festival began in 1959 and today draws an estimated 250,000 people each year to the Village Green. *Garden Grove Historical Society.*

The festival parade, held on Saturday mornings, was illuminated by entertainment stars and other celebrities. Sex symbol Jayne Mansfield was in the 1961 parade, as was Governor Edmund G. "Pat" Brown. Robert Kennedy rode in the 1968 event and spoke to a huge crowd at Bolsa Grande Stadium just a few days before he was assassinated.

Former vice president Hubert Humphrey was in the 1972 parade as part of his bid to win the Democratic presidential nomination that year, and more recent grand marshals have included Clois Leachman, Zsa Zsa Gabor, Mickey Rooney, Shirley Jones, Buddy Hackett and Martin Landau.

Aside from the parades and carnival rides and other fun, the festival serves as a major fundraiser for many local groups as well as for the festival association itself, which has donated millions of dollars to civic and community causes.

With an estimated 250,000 people attending each year, the festival is considered one of the largest of its kind in the western United States; it's certainly the biggest in Orange County.

Left: Academy Award–winning actress Cloris Leachman waves to the crowd while serving as a grand marshal of the Strawberry Festival parade in 2009. *Author's collection.*

Below: Screen legend Mickey Rooney in the 2007 Strawberry Festival parade as celebrity grand marshal. *Author's collection.*

The Strawberry Festival features rides, games, food and entertainment. *Author's collection.*

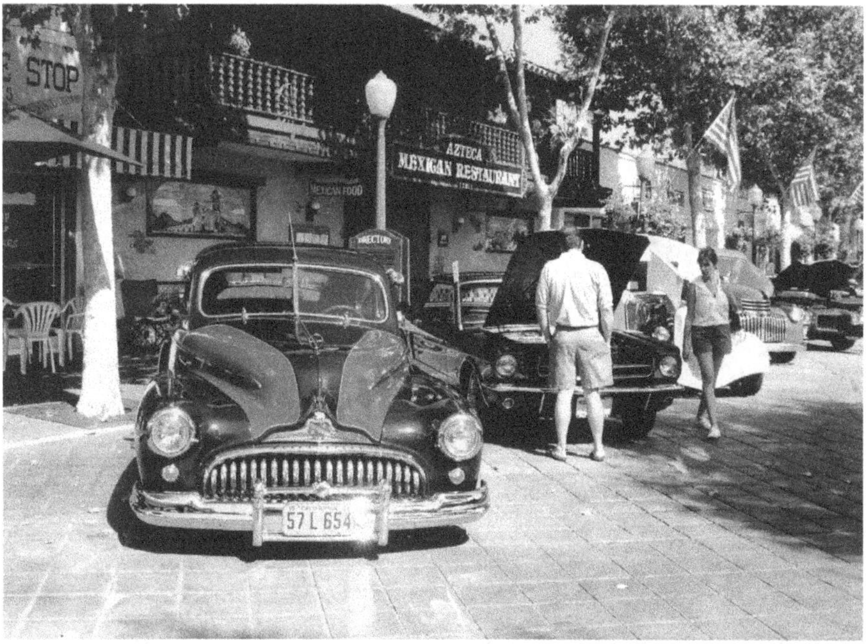

The Strawberry Festival brings visitors to the city's historic Main Street, also well known for its Friday car show. *Author's collection.*

The rapid growth of the population meant huge increases in the number of students in local public schools. Garden Grove High grew so quickly that, in the late 1950s, it was on double sessions. It quickly spun off Rancho Alamitos High in 1957, followed by Bolsa Grande, Santiago, La Quinta, Pacifica and Los Amigos high schools, the latter opening its doors in 1969.

(The GGUSD includes most of Garden Grove and portions of Anaheim, Cypress, Fountain Valley, Santa Ana, Stanton and Westminster. La Quinta is located in Westminster and Los Amigos in Fountain Valley. That portion of Garden Grove east of Haster Street is in the Orange Unified School District, and students there attend Orange High School.)

Struggling to keep up with the surging enrollment, the three school systems serving Garden Grove were building constantly, hiring hundreds of new teachers every year and juggling schools, buses and pupils at a maddening rate.

In 1964, voters in all three districts—Garden Grove elementary, Alamitos elementary and Garden Grove Union High—elected to consolidate the public schools into one system, and the new Garden Grove Unified School District was officially born in 1965.

Garden Grove's diversity is depicted in this image of local high school graduates. *Author's collection.*

Offices of the Garden Grove Unified School District, which in 1965 combined three school systems into one. *Author's collection.*

A mission from the Blessed Sacrament Catholic parish in Westminster turned into the St. Columban Church on Stanford Avenue, the first permanent Catholic church and school in Garden Grove in the mid-1950s. The current larger sanctuary opened in 1967.

A second Catholic church, St. Callistus, opened at Lewis Street and Garden Grove Boulevard in the 1960s. It recently became the home of the Shepherd's Grove congregation, which moved from the Crystal Cathedral in 2013, adopting the new name. The former St. Callistus congregation is now the home parish at the renamed Christ Cathedral.

So many important events took place in this era that the mind blurs watching them sail by—the establishment of the Garden Grove Community Church (forerunner of the Crystal Cathedral) in 1961, local resident Scott Carpenter's trip into space aboard the Liberty 7 space capsule, the controversial purchase of the Dyke Water System in 1965 and the opening of the new regional library in 1969.

But for typical Garden Grovers, the most immediate impacts on their lives came from roads and shops. The new Garden Grove Freeway was dedicated in December 1965, taking the numerical designation of the old Highway 22 from Garden Grove Boulevard and ushering in a new era of access and traffic jams. Many then and now considered the freeway to be a mixed blessing. Even though the new thoroughfare made it easier to get to Garden Grove, it also made it easier to get through the community without stopping and patronizing its businesses or appreciating its charms. Furthermore, the freeway wiped out millions of dollars of assessed valuation and cut into the revenue-strapped city's tax base.

Other street work had its impact. Starting in 1964, several north–south streets were realigned through the city. Stanton and Beach Boulevards were wed into the new Beach Boulevard; Magnolia Street and Cannery Road became Magnolia; Brookhurst and Wright became Brookhurst.

Most significantly, Euclid and Verano Streets were co-joined, which meant the new course of Euclid angled a block east, effectively bypassing the downtown and leading to a decline from which it has only in recent years recovered.

One especially annoying feature of traveling the streets of Garden Grove in the postwar era was flooding. The city grew so fast that little attention was paid to the installation of storm drains. The use of asphalt and concrete meant less rainwater was absorbed into the soil, and water runoff multiplied dramatically.

The result was that when the rains came, Garden Grove flooded. Major intersections were underwater, and some thoroughfares—such as Ninth Street—became notorious for turning into temporary lakes and rivers.

A representative of the Los Angeles Lakers basketball team who drove to the city to speak to a local service club said, "Garden Grove: a swamp with lights."

Eventually, in the 1980s a major storm drain construction program was underway, but there are still areas of the community where a steady downpour (increasingly rare these days) means splashing through wheel-deep water.

In the 1970s, the city contributed, unwittingly, to the downtown's problems. A well-intentioned attempt to spruce up the area had disastrous consequences. Two-thirds of the original central business district was torn down, and much of the land remained vacant for years. Many of the remaining shops fell into disuse or became antique stores. It's only been in recent years that the original heart of Garden Grove has begun to beat with vigor.

For many local residents who could not even name the mayor or identify where the city boundaries were, the most important event of this era might have been the coming of the Orange County Plaza at Chapman Avenue and Brookhurst Street. The land there over time had many uses, including a

Orange County Plaza at Brookhurst Street and Chapman Avenue was the first large shopping center in Orange County. It opened in 1956. *Garden Grove Historical Society.*

pipeworks, and was even planned for a housing development, but it became something else.

Built in phases starting in 1956, the Plaza was once the jewel of retailing for the entire region, and shoppers flocked to the intersection at a pace that latter-day Grovers might consider mythical.

Together with the then-unnamed shopping center (now Pavilion Plaza) at the southwest corner of the crossroads, it made up the new central business district of the community, an area that some called "uptown." Most people just referred to it as "the Plaza."

The Plaza was significant not only for what it was but also for what it was not. From its inception in the Eisenhower era until its decline in the days of Ford and Carter, the center was the leading retail district not just for Garden Grove but also for a surrounding area that included Stanton, Cypress, West Anaheim and Westminster. It could have been a lot bigger.

Initial plans for the center called for two two-story department stores (JC Penney and Newberry's), a farmers' market and dozens of other stores and restaurants, all of it enclosed, according to Louella Kearns, who operated the popular Kandi Kane dress shop from the early days of the Plaza until the late 1980s.

"Don Shandeling and Harry Tinker owned it then," said Kearns, "and they were very successful. Don was very intelligent, a great shopping center man."

He came to California from Minnesota, where the harsh winter climate had given birth to the first enclosed, climate-controlled malls. The Orange County Plaza was going to be California's first.

But piece by piece, the plan unraveled. A planned pedestrian bridge across Chapman Avenue was never built. Newberry's, then a junior department store (a retail classification that has since disappeared), located on the south side of the street in a one-story facility (albeit with a mezzanine) between a new Sav-On drugstore and Vons supermarket.

The Penney store was the anchor for the Plaza, but it was a one-story building, although it had a huge basement that could be used as a second level. The final blow came when Shandeling tried to retrofit the now-outdoor center for his enclosed mall concept.

"A couple of years after it was built," recalled Kearns, "he tried to get the center enclosed. The tenants wouldn't go along because it would have meant higher rents to pay for the air conditioning and remodeling. That's not the way to do it. You don't sign everybody to leases and then afterwards try to get them to agree to something like that."

There were other problems as well. The Plaza really was two centers masquerading as one. The eastern portion was owned by the Chickasawa family of Camarillo, and total ownership of the retail area was split among six owners.

Still, the center prospered. The closest major department store was the Broadway in Anaheim, so most of Garden Grove did its Christmas and back-to-school shopping at Brookhurst and Chapman. The operators of the mall did their part—for a while, anyway—by advertising steadily, staging promotions like car shows regularly and offering a complete mix of shops that included Bank of America, Woolworth's, W.T Grants, Brownie's Toys, Leed's Shoes and Denno's Records. The record store was a major draw for young people; it had such influence it was able to attract the Beach Boys for a live performance.

But signs of danger appeared about a decade after the Plaza's birth, when Orange County got its first enclosed malls, at South Coast Plaza in Costa Mesa and Huntington [Beach] Center (now Bella Terra). As the 1960s segued into the '70s, shoppers flocked to the glitzier enclosed centers, and business at outdoor centers began to sag. For Garden Grove's Plaza, the opening of Westminster Mall in 1974 was probably the tipping point.

Three major attempts have been made to resurrect the Plaza to its former glory. In the late 1970s, under the stewardship of can-do city manager Richard Powers, the City of Garden Grove launched a full-court press against the problem, and for a while, it looked like the city's efforts were going to bear much fruit.

A marketing study by Coldwell Banker called Garden Grove "the hole in the doughnut" with no nearby major malls and suggested that the time might be ripe to expand the plaza and enclose it with a new department store at each end.

For a few weeks in 1978, there were exciting rumors about a new mall with a Montgomery Ward at one end and a Broadway at the other. The possibility of a Buffums store was also raised. Although the city also persuaded the majority owner to sell to the city's favorite—Trans Pacific of Torrance—and contributed $625,000 toward parking lot improvements, the dream died aborning.

Wards seemed a sure bet, with Powers telling a reporter, "We're 99 percent certain" of a deal, but when Mobil purchased the retail chain, the new owner cancelled all expansion plans. Some renovations were made, though, and the former Orange County Plaza (at least the western two-thirds) became Garden Grove Mall in 1980.

In hindsight, the original plan might well have been a misstep. All three of the department stores eyed for the planned mall have gone out of business, and enclosed malls wouldn't last much longer as the open-air center took over in the early twenty-first century.

In 1980, a new exterior, with dark wood facings, seemed to symbolize the skin-deep investment that had been made. The center quickly declined even more sharply to the point that the Pic-N-Save store seemed to be the most successful of the increasingly rare tenants at the mall.

In the late 1980s, the city tried again, helping a new owner consolidate the center under one flag. The new Garden Promenade was redone with the then-popular salmon-and-teal color scheme and with considerable reconstruction—including a Marshall's discount department store—but the center still struggled to attract tenants and keep space leased.

A corner was turned a decade later when the center was renamed the Promenade and boasted the opening of a sixteen-screen Regal Cinema movie complex on the site of the old JC Penney store. With "entertainment centers" all the rage in the early years of the twenty-first century, the arrival of the movie theaters gave a declining retail center a new lease on life.

In recent years, the Promenade has attracted major retailers such as Party City, Petsmart and Ross Dress for Less. Vacancies all but dried up. In the

A sixteen-screen Regal Cinema movie complex is the new anchor for the Promenade, successor to the original Orange County Plaza. *Author's collection.*

summer of 2014, a 107,000-square-foot Walmart department store opened at the west end of the center in the long-empty former Costco building. The thronged parking lot and lines at the movie theater seem to be suggesting that the old "Plaza" might be headed for its own second silver age.

Middle-aged residents (and ex-residents) who grew up in this era might also look back to this time with a silvery sheen. Movie and TV star Steve Martin has been slow to acknowledge his local roots but in one interview conceded that "Garden Grove was a good place to grow up in."

The community was still balanced between its rural past and a fast-moving suburban phase. There were vacant lots and orange groves for kids' adventures. Traffic was lighter; even the new Garden Grove Freeway was wide open for motorists.

Disneyland was just a few minutes to the north, providing both amusement and lots of jobs for young locals. Harbor Boulevard was a popular street to cruise on Saturday night. Friday nights were for high school football and basketball games, and then it was off to Bob's Big Boy or the Pink Spot for refreshment and late dates.

Huntington Beach was a straight shot down Brookhurst Street. Down there was the legendary Golden Bear and the slightly seedy allure of "Surf City." Knott's Berry Farm was a few minutes to the west. And by the mid-

1960s, there was major-league baseball in Anaheim, just a long fly ball from the City of Youth and Ambition.

Boy and Girl Scouts, Little League baseball, Bobby Box softball and Pop Warner football provided skills and memories for many youngsters. Older residents had dozens of civic groups to choose from, ranging from the venerable Garden Grove Lions Club and Women's Civic Club to the now-forgotten Junior Chamber of Commerce and Active 20-30 Club.

There was something for everybody, it seemed. But who those somebodies would be, and how they would last, was just about to change

Chapter 10

THE WORLD RUSHED IN

Of the things that have changed since Garden Grove became more than just a dusty crossroads in a sea of citrus, what's been transformed the most is the population. By 1970, the census figures had leaped to 122,524, a sharp increase over the 1960 figure. But in the decades to come, not only would more people come to the city, but many of them would also arrive from different lands, with different cultures, religions and languages.

Of course, not all of the controversial events of the 1970s and 1980s had to do with the changing demographics of the community. The school system's dress code—no long hair for boys, no pants or short skirts for girls—provoked peaceful but surprising student demonstrations on and off the campuses of several high schools. A series of sit-down protests hit the campuses, and students marched to the offices of the *Orange County Evening News* to publicize their anger. The code was finally jettisoned in 1971 after a ballot box victory by a slate of candidates supported by the teachers' association and many anti–dress code students.

Garden Grove Boulevard—never the toniest part of the community—began to be dotted with adult bookstores and gay bars. The city and its police department battled to control or eliminate these businesses, without much success. For a while, Garden Grove had the dubious distinction of having the most "dirty bookstores" in the county, but what legislation couldn't do, technology did. The home video industry and the Internet took most of the trade away from such shops, and only a few remain across the county.

As the gay rights movement gained acceptance and tolerance, police pressure and community resistance relaxed. At the same time, nightclubs and such catering to the homosexual community went more upscale, and most left for other locations.

The community even gained some notoriety as the first home of *Playgirl* magazine, that publication whose photographs of nude men mirrored the approach of *Playboy*, but for a female audience.

The Playgirl Club was located on Harbor Boulevard just north of Garden Grove Boulevard. It lent its name to the magazine that was founded in 1973 by Douglas Lambert. The nightclub has long since been closed, but the publication still appears monthly. Although originally credited with being emblematic of the women's rights movement, its readership is now believed to be predominately male.

If the devil—or at least the more carnal instincts of the human race—seemed to run triumphant along some local streets, the divine was winning some battles and considerable publicity elsewhere in Garden Grove. From its early days atop a drive-in movie shack stand to a worldwide ministry, the church that would become the Crystal Cathedral made Garden Grove an address known across the nation and planet.

Dr. Robert H. Schuller was born in Alton, Illinois, in 1926. Ordained in 1950 by the Reformed Church in America, Schuller arrived in Garden Grove to start a new church. With his wife, Arvella, playing organ and "$500 in assets," according to Schuller, he rented the nearby Orange Drive-in Theater and conducted Sunday services from the top of that tar paper snack bar.

"It was there I fell in love with the sky," he often said, citing it as inspiration for the all-glass church to come. There was also a small chapel on Chapman Avenue, and the Schullers lived in a modest home nearby. By 1961, he'd financed the construction of the world's first "walk-in, drive-in" church at Lewis Street and Chapman Avenue in the northeastern corner of the city.

The thirteen-story Tower of Hope with its illuminated cross opened in 1968 as the jewel of the rapidly growing Garden Grove Community Church. But there was much more to come.

In 1970, a broadcast of the church's services, *The Hour of Power*, began on one area television station and started Schuller on the road to true international celebrity. Espousing the doctrine of "possibility thinking," which was modeled closely on Dr. Norman Vincent Peale's "Power of Positive Thinking," Schuller decided that an all-glass sanctuary was possible and desirable. In 1981, the spectacular Crystal Cathedral, designed by noted architect Philip Johnson, opened to the applause of architecture critics and churchgoers alike.

Top: Reverend Robert H. Schuller founded the world-famous Crystal Cathedral, now Christ Cathedral. *Author's collection.*

Bottom: The interior of the Crystal Cathedral in Garden Grove. *Orange County Archives.*

Garden Grove's "Koreatown" is located along Garden Grove Boulevard between Brookhurst and Magnolia Streets. *Orange County Archives.*

Some people griped that such an opulent building appealed more to vanity than faith, but the fame of the church spread far and wide to the point that it became one of Orange County's leading tourist attractions. The building can be seen by motorists on the Garden Grove and Orange freeways.

The cathedral was also home to the annual "Glory of Easter" and "Glory of Christmas" pageants, and Schuller became the confidante and counselor of presidents, Hollywood celebrities and even Soviet premiers. Although religious broadcasters (sometimes derided as "television evangelists") lost some influence in the 1980s in a wave of sex scandals, Schuller remained above the fray, presiding over his ten-thousand-member church and multimillion-person audience.

But nothing stays the same, and Schuller and the church he founded—as we will see in a later chapter—eventually were humbled.

In 1981, when the glass church opened, Garden Grove was still very much a "white folks" community. The census that year showed its 125,900 population to be 85 percent white, 10 percent Latino and 5 percent Asian. But that was all about to change.

Political unrest in Korea led to the establishment of Korean communities across the Pacific Rim, including a new business district in Garden Grove. Centered where the old Garden Square once held court as a thriving center, the new "Koreatown" served as a shopper's paradise for Koreans living in Orange County.

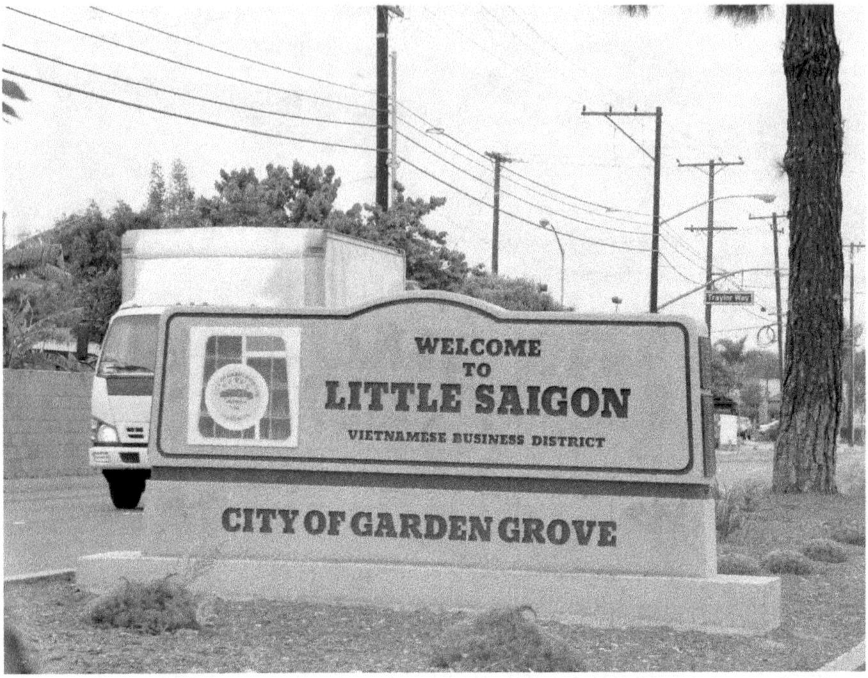

This sign on Brookhurst Street south of Trask Avenue signals the start of Garden Grove's Little Saigon area. *Author's collection.*

The sudden appearance of signs in Korean lettering along the city's namesake street provoked considerable grumbling, and one city councilman even proposed that all signs be in English. He was told that such a law would likely be held unconstitutional and even lead to such absurdities as forcing a chain hot dog eatery to go by the name "Veal Cutlet."

Garden Grove's first taste of diversity became an entire meal by the early 1980s. After the fall of Saigon in 1975, thousands of Indochinese refugees (mostly Vietnamese) fled the advance of communism. Many were evacuated by U.S. forces to Camp Pendleton in San Diego County. The willingness of churches and other social agencies in Garden Grove and Westminster to offer help attracted many to those cities.

It wasn't long before large numbers of Vietnamese began to move to Orange County from wherever they had been first settled and the tensions that almost always arise when a new ethnic group comes to town began to surface.

"Will the last American in Garden Grove please take the American flag?" asked one bumper sticker. Indeed, the speed at which unfamiliar languages and skin tones appeared created a testy atmosphere and apprehension that redounded not entirely to Garden Grove's credit.

It may have been morning in America in the 1980s, but Garden Grove was in a funk. Bypassed by malls and movie theaters, subject to growing ethnic tensions and gang problems and stalled by a constantly feuding city council, it seemed to be a city without vision or much of a future. White flight to the paler districts of South Orange County drew away some of the population while the uneven economic atmosphere of the times undercut many development efforts. More and more often, people outside of the community used the epithet "Garbage Grove" despite the best efforts of local government and agencies to polish the image.

In 1979, the passage of Proposition 13 by California voters shifted the burden of supporting municipal services from property taxes to sales tax, further exposing just how precarious local civic finances were.

At the southeastern tip of the city, in the Buena-Clinton area of decaying apartment houses, the *Los Angeles Times* found "the worst slum in Orange County." Stung into action, the city government moved to improve the area, but not before Garden Grove's name was associated with blight all across Southern California. The presence of the slum was no surprise. Police called it "Scab Acres," in reference to the number of residents using illegal intravenous drugs. The problems there had long been reported by civic groups and the local press, but it took regional embarrassment to get effective action.

Garden Grove has also suffered through a series of deaths by on-duty police officers, five in all (the most in Orange County). The most recent was Howard Dallies Jr., fatally shot in a traffic stop in 1992. Each year, a somber memorial observance, "Call to Duty," remembers those fallen officers.

There were successes, however. Euclid Park, the city's first, was doubled in size and renamed the Village Green. A new Civic Center Park, complete with ponds, waterfalls, bridges and ducks, was created at Stanford Avenue and Euclid Street, adjacent to the regional library and the new Community Meeting Center.

The Gem Theatre, originally a vaudeville and movie house dating from the Roaring Twenties, closed its doors on Main Street in 1971. But in 1979, it was renovated for use for the staging of live theater. A 550-seat outdoor Festival Amphitheater was built next door in the Village Green Park, and together they hosted the critically acclaimed Grove Shakespeare Festival.

On formerly unused strips of dirt alongside the Garden Grove Freeway on Trask Avenue, the city planted a new Garden Grove Auto Center, which

Each year, the "Call to Duty" service memorializes the five Garden Grove police officers killed in the line of duty. *Author's collection.*

is now home to six new car dealerships. The Auto Center has been a major contributor to city tax revenue.

The former Nike antiaircraft missile site on the west side was turned into a 215-acre centrally planned, beautifully landscaped light industrial park. There was some controversy over that decision. Some residents lobbied for the creation of a regional park; others suggested a shopping center would be a good choice.

But before Proposition 13 passed in 1979, the principal source of civic revenue was property tax, and industrial uses brought in the best return. Afterward, sales tax became the key, and cities competed with one another to attract retail and automotive businesses in order to help balance the books. Car dealerships, shopping centers and big-box retailers such as Costco and Home Depot were eagerly sought.

After stalling, the city's population began to grow again, reaching 130,319 by 1985 and booming to 142,975 by the 1990 census.

The city's first major department store, Mervyn's (now Burlington), opened at Harbor and Garden Grove Boulevards, and the aging Palm Harbor Hospital was replaced with a modern Garden Grove Hospital and Medical Center.

In the mid-1980s, the city's redevelopment agency successfully landed the community's first major hotel, the fourteen-story Princess Alicante (now

Top: The Gem Theater on Main Street, dating from the silent film era, was closed as a movie house in 1971 and reopened as a live stage theater. The above image shows how the theater looked in 1974. *Orange County Archives.*

Bottom: The Gem Theater reopened in 1979 as a live-stage theater. *Garden Grove Historical Society.*

Hyatt Regency Orange County) at Chapman and Harbor. It would be a harbinger of more to come.

As time passed, ethnic tensions seemed to ease, and almost without much public notice, the Hispanic population of the city began to grow significantly, reflecting a trend happening all across Orange County.

The last decade of the century saw Garden Grove on the proverbial edge, poised to tip into abyss and disrepute or move forward into a new era of progress and success. As always, this course of this phase of history turned on a combination of national trends and local change.

Chapter 11

THE TURNING POINT

To be a Garden Grove loyalist in 1990 required something more than just local pride; you might even need a gas mask and a set of earplugs. Public wrangling over the Great Bard and the tiny Medfly seemed to symbolize how unlucky the city had been in changing an image that some regarded as tarnished.

It's easy to think of California as a state full of movie stars, beaches, suburbs and freeways, but it's also one of the most important agricultural regions in the United States. When the Mediterranean fruit fly (otherwise known as the "Medfly"), a major threat to the Golden State's agribusiness, was found in Orange County in 1990, helicopters and politicians sprang into action.

Under prodding from major growers, the state launched a Medfly eradication program that took a dramatic turn. Helicopters fitted out with large outboard chemical tanks flew low over Garden Grove and other communities, spraying the insecticide Malathion in an effort to stop the threat.

The spraying prompted a public outcry. The eerie sound of the 'copters overhead on Thursday nights sent a shiver down many Garden Grove spines, and some complained that the spray made breathing difficult and damaged the paint on their cars. City Councilman Ray Littrell was among the leaders of opposition to the spraying. The aerial warfare was eventually called off, but the whole episode did little to encourage the idea that the community was a desirable place to live.

More public rebuke emerged on the cultural front. The Grove Shakespeare Festival (GSF), long subsidized by the city, saw its funding cut and then eliminated as some members of the city council objected both to the GSF's subsidy and the allegedly arcane content of Shakespeare's work.

From the public debate that followed in the council chambers and on TV and in the press, one might develop the opinion that in Garden Grove, high culture was in as much danger as the Medfly.

Those issues played out against a backdrop of political and economic frustration. Many efforts to redevelop keys area of the city—especially the downtown area—bore little or no fruit. The sluggish national economy drew developers only to the trendiest and surest-seeming locations, which did not include west central Orange County.

Political infighting added to the problem. When Mayor Jon Cannon resigned to take a judgeship in 1987, the rest of the city council couldn't agree on a replacement, making a special election necessary. Former mayor J.T. Tilman Williams won narrowly and then was defeated in 1988 by Walt Donovan, giving Garden Grove three mayors in a year's time.

Further, the council was split into a pro-redevelopment wing and those opposed. While the "pro" forces were always in the majority, they sometimes lacked the two-thirds support necessary to invoke the power of eminent domain, a powerful, if sometimes misused, weapon against blight.

In the local public schools, test scores reflected the many languages spoken in GGUSD homes. Critics who looked at those numbers compared then–lily white upper-class Irvine, for example, with diverse Garden Grove and decided that local schools weren't good enough.

And yet...and yet, underneath it all was a faint undercurrent of change for the better, which would eventually echo louder and more strongly. The national economy had begun to improve by 1993. In the 1994 city council election, a new majority of pro-redevelopment members was chosen, led by Mayor Bruce Broadwater, who would go on to become the city's longest-serving top elected official. The result was a political unity that would ease the gridlock at city hall.

New political and economic winds began to blow. Reflecting perhaps a new appreciation of colorblindness, Garden Grove's first Asian American city councilman—Ho Chung—was elected. The *Garden Grove Journal*, founded in 1983, became a strong force for energetic city action on a variety of fronts, even urging readers to support tax measures and school bond issues with front-page banners.

A new majority on the school board pushed for a return to basics. Others said the district never abandoned them, but still the sterner standards promised—and have seemed to deliver—higher test scores.

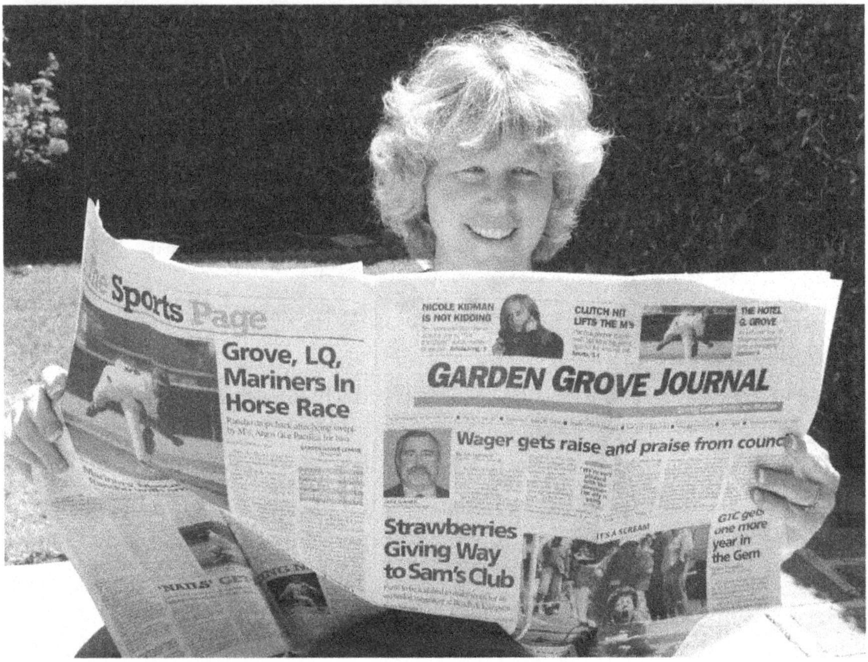

Top: Bruce Broadwater is Garden Grove's longest-serving mayor. *Author's collection.*

Bottom: Marilyn Lewis Tortolano (wife of the author) reads the hometown newspaper, *Garden Grove Journal*. *Author's collection.*

Laura Schwalm, the Garden Grove school system's first female superintendent. *Author's collection.*

The board followed that by making history in hiring the local school system's first female superintendent, the respected Dr. Laura Schwalm. Under her leadership, student performance increased dramatically, and in 2006, the GGUSD won the Broad Prize as the best urban school district in the United States.

Crime began to decline after 1990 and went on a run of annual reductions that persists even today. The gang and graffiti problems that once seemed ready to consume the community were reduced dramatically.

One event that pushed Garden Grove into the national limelight was the murder of O.J. Simpson's ex-wife, Nicole Brown Simpson, in 1994. She had spent her early years in Garden Grove, attending local schools, including Rancho Alamitos High School, before her family moved to Dana Hills after her sophomore year.

Simpson, in what has been called the "Trial of the Century," was acquitted of the murder charges (he was also accused of killing his wife's friend Ronald Goldman) but was found responsible for her "wrongful death" in 1997 in a $40 million lawsuit. Simpson, a famed professional football player, was later arrested and convicted of armed robbery charges in Nevada and was sentenced to thirty-three years in prison in 2008. He will be eligible for parole in 2017.

Through the 1990s, the leadership of City Manager George Tindall and Community Development Director Matt Fertal helped the city move aggressively to woo and win developers for a variety of sites. The once moribund downtown became home to popular big-box retailers Costco, Home Depot and Office Depot. A new Higher Education Center offering classes through Cal State Fullerton and Coastline Community College opened in gleaming buildings at the corner of Euclid Street and Garden Grove Boulevard.

The original city hall, first built in 1923 as Washington Grammar School, was demolished as city offices moved into a modern three-story facility two blocks west.

With Disneyland planning a major expansion (California Adventure), Harbor Boulevard became an attractive location for development. Although plans for two entertainment centers—E-Street and Riverwalk—never came to fruition, hotels fared better. No fewer than eight new high- and mid-rise hotels sprouted in the Harbor Corridor, bringing with them chain restaurants such as Outback Steakhouse, Red Robin, Joe's Crab Shack and Buca di Beppo.

Housing starts boomed as well by the mid-1990s, and by decade's end, new single-family housing tracts were popping up all over Garden Grove, the largest being a 136-home upscale project on one of the last of the community's large strawberry fields at Chapman and Euclid.

At his 1998 State of the City address, Mayor Broadwater wrote finis to the way things had been.

"Goodbye to strawberry fields and provincialism," he said. "That's not Garden Grove anymore."

Chapter 12

NEW CITY FOR A NEW CENTURY

The twenty-first century had a rough, tragic, trying start for all of America, including Garden Grove. It wasn't long into the new millennium that the terrorist attack on the United States by Al-Qaeda swiftly ended the sunny mood on which the previous century had ended.

Like most other communities, Garden Grove residents mourned and rallied together. A candlelight observance lent a somber tone to the Friday Night Car Show on Main Street. The city organized a more formal memorial in the Civic Center, marked by prayer and patriotism. A huge American flag was unfurled along the front of the Public Safety building on Acacia Parkway. Thousands of people attended in a show of community unity that crossed all ethnic, religious and political lines. For one evening in September 2011, the city and the nation seemed like a more perfect union.

Of course, not every person could find the common cause in his or her heart. Some people made threats against the mosque and school run by the Islamic Society of Orange County, located on Thirteenth Street in Garden Grove. Police prudently provided extra patrols and security there, and no serious incidents occurred.

The attacks on 9/11 pushed the United States into war against Saddam Hussein's Iraq and Taliban-dominated Afghanistan. More than a decade later, American armed forces were still in action in both countries despite the defeat of both tyrannical regimes. The war drew Garden Grovers in, and like most wars, it had its heroes and villains.

Born in 1981, Michael Anthony Monsoor was a local boy who played tight end on the Garden Grove High School football team, graduating in 1999. He enlisted in the U.S. Navy in 2001 and entered the elite SEALS commando program, finally finishing his grueling training in 2005.

Assigned to Delta Platoon, SEAL Team 3, he went to Iraq in April 2006 to train Iraqi soldiers. While there, he fought in many encounters with insurgent forces. He was honored with a Silver Star and Bronze Star for heroism.

On September 29, he and other SEALS (along with three Iraqi soldiers) were on a rooftop after a firefight. A hand grenade was thrown onto the roof, hitting Monsoor in the chest. It fell to the ground. Monsoor shouted, "Grenade!" and jumped on the device, shielding his comrades from most of the force of the blast. He died from his wounds.

For his actions, Monsoor was awarded the Medal of Honor, the highest decoration in the American military. His medal was presented to his parents by President George W. Bush on April 8, 2008. A guided missile destroyer (under construction as we go to print) will be named after Monsoor.

The other Garden Grover whose name surfaced during this decade of war was famous for being seen as a traitor, not a selfless patriot. Adam Gadahn was born Adam Pearlman and grew up in rural Riverside County. His family moved to Santa Ana, and although raised as a Christian, he eventually developed an interest in Islam, converting to that faith around 1995. He attended the Islamic Society of Orange County's mosque in Garden Grove and lived for a while in the city. He clashed with the moderate mosque leadership and was arrested and convicted of assault there.

Gadahn, also known as Azzam al-Amriki ("Azzam the American"), is believed to have moved to Pakistan in 1998 and was soon connected to Al-Qaeda, the group blamed for the terrorist attacks on 9/11. He became a key part of Osama Bin Laden's organization and began making anti-American videos. He was charged with treason in 2006 and has been sought by the FBI since 2004, with a $1 million reward for his arrest or conviction. The first American to be officially charged with treason in over half a century, he could face the death penalty if apprehended and convicted.

Garden Grove also made national news as a first generation of Vietnamese American officeholders made their way into positions of government. Janet Nguyen broke two barriers in 2004 when she was not only the first Vietnamese to be elected to the city council but also the first woman elected to that post in over three decades.

In 2006, Orange County supervisor Lou Correa was elected to the state senate, creating a vacancy in the First District seat, which includes Santa Ana,

Janet Nguyen's election to the Garden Grove City Council and Orange County Board of Supervisors signaled the rising prominence of the Vietnamese community. *Author's collection.*

Garden Grove and Westminster. In a special election that demonstrated the growing election day influence of the Vietnamese community, Janet Nguyen edged Trung Nguyen, a member of the Garden Grove school board, by a total of three votes once a recount was completed. She was easily reelected in 2008 and in 2012. A Republican, in 2014 she ran for thirty-fourth state Senate district seat and defeated her Democratic opponent, Jose Solario, by a wide margin.

Her success in climbing the electoral ladder was mirrored by other successes for other Vietnamese American candidates. As this book goes to print, there are two city council members of Vietnamese heritage (Dina Nguyen and Chris Phan) and two school board members (Lan Nguyen and Bao Nguyen). Bao Nguyen ran for mayor in November 2014 and unseated the incumbent mayor, Bruce Broadwater, in a very close election.

The Tet Festival, held every year in Garden Grove Park, is second only to the Strawberry Festival in attendance.

Less visible but numerically larger is the growth of the Hispanic community. According to recent demographic estimates, about 40 percent of Garden Grove residents are Hispanic (mostly of Mexican descent). Asians and Pacific Islanders are around 37 percent (mostly Vietnamese and Korean), with non-Hispanic whites about 23 percent. That bulge in population has not yet translated into political power, as far fewer Hispanics have become naturalized citizens than Asians.

Another shift in the landscape of leadership was the rise of women into positions of power in the community. Janet Nguyen was followed on the city council by Dina Nguyen. GGUSD superintendent Laura Schwalm, who

The lion dance is one of many colorful traditions at the Tet Festival in Garden Grove. *Author's collection.*

stepped down in 2013, was succeeded in that post by Gabriela Mafi. Meanwhile, Pat Halberstadt presided over the Boys and Girls Club of Garden Grove, which expanded under her care to be the largest in Orange County. Other women rose to top administrative roles in the city and school district, and Loretta Sanchez (D-Garden Grove) has served in the House of Representatives since 1994.

Another big impact on Garden Grove was the Great Recession, which began in 2007–08 and whose effects still linger today. The collapse of the housing market and the credit crisis threw millions out of work and stopped many local developments cold.

In the years running up to that downturn, Garden Grove made some strides in a wide variety of areas. Funding was found for parks improvements, including a new gymnasium, dog park and skateboarding spot in Garden Grove Park. A new Garden Grove Conference Center was built adjacent to the Hyatt Regency hotel, giving the city a convention center that attracted conclaves from all over,

The Festival Amphitheater is host to the professional Shakespeare Orange County troupe. This photograph depicts a performance of *Othello*. *Author's collection.*

including the Republican state convention one year.

The two city-owned theaters in the Village Green Park, the Gem and the Festival Amphitheater, got new life as energetic operators moved in. Shakespeare Orange County, brainchild of Thomas Bradac (who had founded the original Grove Shakespeare Festival in 1979), returned to the outdoor amphitheater in 2004. One More Productions brought its lineup of musical comedy performances to the Gem in 2008.

However, the earthquake that was the capital-R recession slammed local institutions hard. Budgets for the City of Garden Grove and school district, along with many Orange County institutions, were ravaged, leading to layoffs, hiring freezes and, in some cases, pay cuts in the form of furloughs. The school year was trimmed, and unemployment in the city surged past 10 percent, a figure not seen since such records were kept.

While the Great Recession didn't bring bread lines to the city as the Great Depression had, it did strain local resources for the relief of the jobless and homeless and call a halt to some projects planned for the community.

But to a remarkable degree, the near-crash nevertheless saw important progress made. Despite the lingering effects of the downturn, the GGUSD proposed and won voter approval for the passage of Measure A, the first school bond issue approved locally in a half century. Voters backed a $250 million school modernization program to repair and improve the school system's aging campuses, many of which were fifty or more years old. One building at Garden Grove High dated back to the 1920s. Measure A, backed strongly by various employee and civic groups and the *Garden Grove Journal*, won with 59.8 percent of the vote. To pass, the bond issue needed 55 percent.

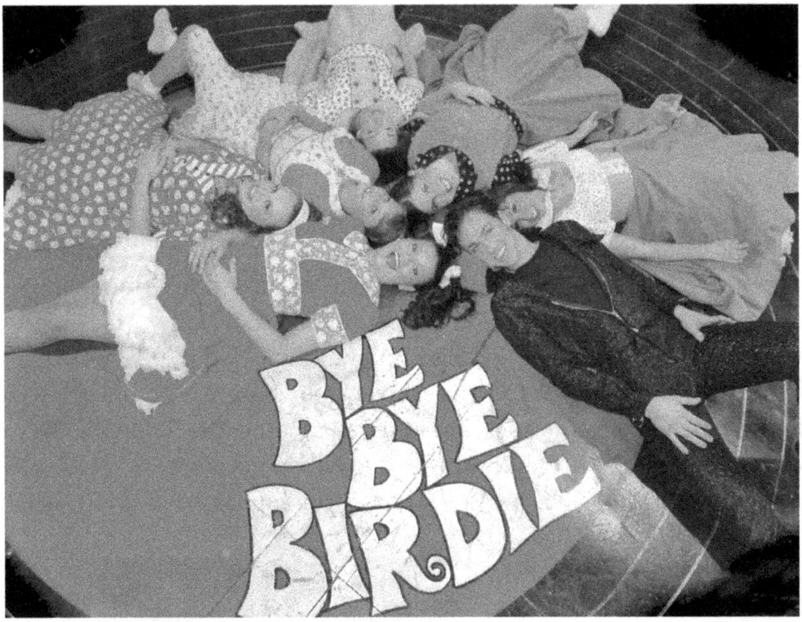

One More Productions is the resident company at the Gem Theater. Pictured here is a scene from *Bye Bye Birdie*. *Author's collection.*

Through the considerable skill of chief financial officer Sue McCann, the bond issue's financial impact was nearly doubled through the winning of various state and federal grants. Virtually every school in the district will undergo extensive work, and construction and reconstruction is continuing as this book is written.

In Garden Grove's third century, there were some big plans and some big duds. Some grand projects took root, and some died aborning.

The proposal that brought the most potential for change—and the greatest controversy—was the idea of a huge casino–entertainment complex on a thirty-five-acre plot at Garden Grove and Harbor Boulevards.

Just before the Great Recession's leading waves hit in 2007–08, a tantalizing prospect of riches appeared. The Gabrielino-Tongva tribe of Native Americans, fronted by development director Jonathan Stein, proposed the $1 billion project for Garden Grove, just a few miles south of family-friendly Disneyland.

"If the project were built," Stein said in 2007, "we would be the biggest tax generator in the state." Tribes have a special legal status as "domestic nations" and in some instances are able to sponsor projects such as casinos, which are otherwise banned or restricted in California.

The proposal actually called for two casinos with up to 7,500 slot machines and two hundred game tables. Additionally, it would have included two "upper up-scale [*sic*]" hotel towers with one thousand rooms.

But that's not all. Also foreseen was a stadium seating up to ten thousand people for sporting events, concerts and community cultural events and two theaters (one of seven hundred to one thousand seats and another with three hundred to five hundred seats) for smaller concerts and local culture, including live theater.

The list went on: five specialty venues (dance clubs/discos, nightclubs and lounges), up to fourteen restaurants, two twenty-hour buffets, fifty specialty stores, a multi-screen movie complex and more.

In exchange for Garden Grove agreeing to host the complex—which, technically, would become part of a reservation—the tribe offered to pay the city $100 million up front and provide annual tax payments of $124 million or more. Additionally, the casino would pay an annual fee of $10 million to the Garden Grove Unified School District and create a scholarship fund to send each GGUSD graduate to college.

The Great Wolf Hotel and Water Park is under construction on Harbor Boulevard and is slated for opening in 2016. *Author's collection.*

Despite the promised largess, the idea sparked a strong negative reaction from several quarters, especially the Vietnamese community. Hundreds turned out to beseech the council to reject the proposal, claiming the casino project would increase crime and problems with gambling addictions.

"I have seen firsthand the effects of the problem," said Councilwoman Dina Nguyen. On September 11, 2007, the council voted 5–0 to instead select McWhinney Enterprise's proposal to build a partially enclosed water park, along with retail and meeting space.

The recession that followed would slow development along what the city wanted to brand as "International West," a California riff on the entertainment district in Orlando, Florida. Further complicating conditions was a new state law enacted in 2011 that abolished redevelopment agencies.

First created in the late 1940s to assist in urban renewal, redevelopment agencies came into wide use in the 1970s and '80s, helping cities to build improvements and lure developers. But controversies over the use and abuse of the eminent domain power arose. Additionally, the agencies took tax money that otherwise would have gone to city general funds, as well as school districts.

But Garden Grove was less affected than some communities. "We have existing obligations, which will last for years," said city manager Matt Fertal, allowing the city to proceed with pending projects such as the water park hotel and other developments in the Harbor area, now called the Grove District portion of the Anaheim Resort.

Skirmishes over land use and development continued here and there. A proposal in 2007 to build a huge Walmart store on the south side of Chapman Avenue west of Brookhurst generated a storm of controversy, and despite city council approval, the project was dropped. Six years later, a plan to build a smaller Walmart on the north side of Chapman prompted no protests, and the store opened in the summer of 2014.

The parking lot west of the city's historic Main Street became the focus of another battle. A developer wanted to build a condo complex on the land but was opposed by the Garden Grove Downtown Business Association. A lawsuit ensued, but although the developer prevailed in court, the coming of the recession made the project unfeasible, and the parking lot remains.

Perhaps the most bizarre and well-publicized crime in Garden Grove history took place in July 2011, when an angry woman drugged her estranged husband, cut off his penis and threw it down a running garbage disposal. In April 2013, Catherine Kieu was convicted on charges of torture and aggravated mayhem. She was reportedly angry because her husband had gone back to seeing his ex-girlfriend. Kieu was sentenced to seven years to life in state prison in July 2013.

A tragedy at a high school football game in 2009 not only united the community but also focused national attention on safety issues associated with the sport. In the opening game of the Garden Grove High School football season, the visiting Argonauts held a 9–0 lead over the host Westminster Lions. Running back Kevin Telles ripped off a long run for the Argos with 2:16 to play in the game and then collapsed on the field. Attempts to revive him failed, and he was taken to a Huntington Beach hospital, where he was pronounced dead of heart failure.

Telles's death led to much publicity about how to prevent health problems in the strenuous sport of tackle football. One result was the widespread use of cardiac pre-screening for high school athletes.

Dedicating the season to Telles, the team went on to advance to the CIF Southern Section finals for the first time since 1945. Two years later, the Argonauts would win the first CIF-SS football title in the school's history, winning a nail-biter 31–30 over Beckman High School. The team's star player, Josh Webb, was named Orange County Player of the Year.

More national attention came to Garden Grove as the world-famous Crystal Cathedral became the site of controversy, bankruptcy and, eventually, a sale. The all-glass sanctuary was a landmark since its opening in 1981, but the Great Recession and a change in churchgoing habits took its toll on the famous ministry in the new century. Contributions declined, and the congregation dwindled. Rough economic times reduced the take at the collection plate, and the traditional aspects of the services attracted a smaller, older crowd.

By 2010, vendors and creditors of Crystal Cathedral Ministries had filed lawsuits, complaining about unpaid bills. In October, the church filed for bankruptcy, claiming it was $43 million in debt.

Josh Webb led Garden Grove High School to its first-ever CIF football championship in 2010, edging Beckman High, 31–30. *Author's collection.*

The financial woes of the ministry mirrored its internal difficulties. Founder Robert H. Schuller appointed his son as successor in 2006 and then changed his mind in 2010 and ousted Robert A. Schuller, replacing him with Sheila Schuller Coleman, the founder's daughter.

Placing the church campus up for sale attracted several bidders, including Chapman University and the Roman Catholic Diocese of Orange. The diocese was the winner, agreeing to pay $57.5 million for the complex, which included a cemetery, a prayer tower, office buildings and the Tower of Hope, in addition to the cathedral.

The sanctuary has been renamed Christ Cathedral, and the former Crystal Cathedral congregation has been relocated to the former campus of St. Callistus Catholic Church on Lewis Street in Garden Grove, a mile to the south. The move took place in July 2013. The relocated ministry is called Shepherd's Grove. Bobby Schuller, grandson of the founder, is the pastor and is continuing the broadcast of *Hour of Power* worldwide.

For locals, though, much of the news for Garden Grove has centered on two other streets in town: Harbor Boulevard and Main Street. As mentioned above, the city has been laboring to transform Harbor from a patchwork of stores, houses and empty lots into a glittering entertainment thoroughfare.

While the hotel cluster at Chapman Avenue was a start, the long-delayed Great Wolf water park hotel project was considered a major step toward getting attractions in the city and not just relying on the Disney Resort area to attract visitors. The Great Wolf project, with an enclosed year-round water recreation area, broke ground in 2014, and completion is expected by 2016.

Farther up the street on the east side of Harbor, the next major planned development would be Grove Towers, consisting of one high-rise and another mid-rise hotel in a project that will include 769 rooms, thirty-nine thousand square feet of conference and meeting space and forty-five thousand feet of commercial space, which could include restaurants and stores.

When those are completed, the total number of major hotels in the Grove District will stand at twelve, with more development foreseen all the way down Harbor to the city limit with Santa Ana.

In fact, Santa Ana and Garden Grove might soon be drawn into a steely embrace. Santa Ana is planning the construction of a streetcar line that will connect from its downtown west to a station on Harbor in Garden Grove near Westminster Avenue. A portion of the route would run along the long-abandoned Pacific Electric right of way of Red Car fame.

To further inflame the imaginations of rail fans, Anaheim is considering its own streetcar project to the north. Some at city hall in Garden Grove can envision snaking a rail line down Harbor, connecting downtown Santa Ana to the Disney Resort and possibly Angel Stadium and Honda Center, right through the City of Youth and Ambition.

If that came to pass, it wouldn't be impossible for the remainder of the PE right of way to be used for a rail line that could, for example, connect the Brookhurst-Chapman area. Imagine being able to step onto a streetcar by the Regal Cinema and read a book or magazine while you are whisked to an Angels game in Anaheim or Bowers Museum in Santa Ana.

But just as much attention is now being focused on where Garden Grove all began. The original, tiny village at Ocean Boulevard and the Anaheim Road turned into a town and then a city. Realignments, freeways, neglect and more made the downtown area more of a curiosity than a center.

However, in an era where city cores are now booming, a new effort is being made to revive and expand Garden Grove's original central business district. Plans are still being made, but a concept of extending Main Street through the Village Green Park to connect to Euclid Street has been advanced. The city owns several properties east of Euclid in the Civic Center area, so an amalgamation of downtown and public buildings is possible.

Planners can imagine a new central Garden Grove with sidewalk cafés, art galleries, apartments and condos above street-level businesses and other amenities that are attracting seniors and hipsters alike to walkable, historic places. The "Reimagine Downtown" effort is aimed at making the city's birthplace appealing, lively and prosperous.

There are already signs of big change there. The Century Village condo complex just north of Main Street sold out quickly, and developers are interested in building new housing for downtown residents who would need the services and amenities an expanded commercial district could provide.

The success of an entertainment corridor in the Grove District and a homey, slow-paced strollable city center would give Garden Grove the best of two worlds: places to have fun late into the night and spots to sip coffee quietly with old friends under a leafy canopy. Bright lights and cool breezes.

Another change in the city gathering steam is the change in the housing stock. A classic "bedroom community," most of the homes were ranch-style single-family homes constructed in the 1950s and '60s on relatively large lots, land being cheap then. The style was the embodiment of the American dream: lush lawns in the front; spacious backyards for kids, pools and barbecues; and two-car garages.

Two forces are working to change that. Some developers (and some individuals) have begun buying up the homes on large lots, tearing down

The Century Village project downtown reflects a move toward growing urbanization in Garden Grove. *Author's collection.*

the buildings and constructing either imposing mansions of two stories and five or six bedrooms or closely built modern condominiums or town houses.

Reflecting modern trends, virtually all the new housing built in Garden Grove is of the two-story variety, with small—even tiny—backyards.

The other wave hitting the city is the coming of mid- and high-rise housing. All across Orange County, apartment or condominium buildings of five to ten stories are going up, and Garden Grove will soon join their ranks. The four-story Chapman Commons (west of Harbor Boulevard) will soon be joined by a ten-story condo complex in the Brookhurst Triangle, an area formed by the confluence of Garden Grove Boulevard, Brookhurst Way and Brookhurst Street.

Slowly, and perhaps surely, Garden Grove is acquiring a more urbanized look, and the open spaces and low-slung appearances of the past are giving way to a new twenty-first-century American dream of vibrant city life based not so much around cars as around public transit and mixed-use development, which will put commercial uses such as markets and restaurants close by housing.

Looking over the long history of this community, it's gone through many changes, with times of rapid progress and slow growth. There have been spurts and setbacks, but it is always moving forward. There have been golden and silver ages before, so who's to say we're not at the edge of a new period of greatness?

There's an old saying claiming, "If you wait long enough, everything comes back into style." From high-rises on Harbor to cobblestones on Main Street, it's very possible that Garden Grove is coming back into style as well.

As Garden Grove heads into the future, you might say that the whole community is pulling together. *Author's collection.*

Many local groups are represented in the annual Strawberry Festival parade. *Author's collection.*

Appendix I

GARDEN GROVE TIMELINE

1784: The land grant of Rancho Las Bolsas is granted by the king of Spain.
1822: Mexico wins independence from Spain.
1848: The United States wins the Mexican War, and California becomes part of the United States after the signing of the Treaty of Guadalupe Hildalgo.
1860: Abel Stearns buys much of the original land grants in the Santa Ana Valley area.
1861: Floods, followed by drought, wipe out the cattle-grazing business in area.
1868: Alfred Robinson buys Stearns's holdings, and subdivisions begin.
1869: John Mitchell, the first permanent settler in Garden Grove, arrives.
1874: Alonzo Gerry Cook arrives, establishing the Garden Grove community, including a church, a public school and businesses.
1880 (or 1881): Cook leaves Garden Grove.
1889: The Santa Ana Valley area (including Garden Grove) votes to separate from Los Angeles County, establishing Orange County.
1905: The Pacific Electric railway system comes to Garden Grove, connecting the community with the outside world and establishing it as a key location for shipping produce, including citrus.
1907: The Garden Grove Improvement Association (now the Chamber of Commerce) is founded.
1909: *Garden Grove News* begins publishing. The first issue is four pages.
1911: The first public streetlights come to what's now Main Street.
1912: First paved street (also Main Street).

1916: The Santa Ana River overflows, flooding much of Garden Grove. Residents dynamite a raised railway to relieve downtown flooding.
1916: The first attempt to incorporate as a city fails.
1921: Garden Grove Union High School District is established; Garden Grove High School opens in temporary quarters in September.
1922: The second attempt to incorporate a city is voted down 227–186.
1924: The Garden Grove Sanitary District established.
1927: The Garden Grove Fire Protection District established.
1930: The third attempt to incorporate as a city is voted down 359–262.
1933: The Long Beach Earthquake strikes, leveling much of Garden Grove's central business district. A student at Garden Grove High School is killed by falling debris. The Euclid Improvement Association organizes rebuilding of downtown with a Spanish mission motif, as well as a widening of Euclid Street.
1940–41: The Garden Grove Sanitarium and Greenbrier Inn are established on Garden Grove Boulevard.
1941: The Japanese attack on Pearl Harbor results in the relocation of hundreds of Japanese residents from Garden Grove.
1944 : A prisoner-of-war camp for German POWs is established in Garden Grove and closed in 1946. Later, it is used as a camp for bracero "guest" farm workers from Mexico.
1944: Haster Air Field is established by the U.S. Navy. The site is now occupied by Garden Grove Park and Bolsa Grande High School.
1945: Garden Grove High football team loses 12–6 to Downey High in the CIF Southern Section championship game. (Actually, because of wartime travel restrictions, the four league champions played just one playoff contest, with the winners declared co-champs and the losers co-runners-up).
1946: The state court rules that the segregation of Mexican children into separate schools (as practiced in elementary schools in Garden Grove, El Modena, Santa Ana and Westminster) is unconstitutional. *Mendez v. Westminster* serves as a precedent for *Brown v. Board of Education*, in which the U.S. Supreme Court held that "separate but equal" school systems were unconstitutional.
1948: Snowfall comes to Garden Grove, covering much of the community with an unusual layer of white.
1955: The fourth attempt to incorporate as a city is voted down 2,835–2,465.
1955: Reverend Robert H. Schuller begins his "drive-in" ministry.
1956: A fifth attempt to incorporate as a city is approved 5,780–2,346. City population is estimated at forty-four thousand. H. Louis Lake is Garden Grove's first mayor.

1956: The first phase of Orange County Plaza opens at Brookhurst Street and Chapman Avenue.
1956: *Garden Grove News* goes daily and becomes the *Daily News*. It will later be named the *News* (to avoid confusion with the *Orange Daily News*) and, in 1964, the *Orange County Evening News*.
1959: The first Strawberry Festival is held.
1960: Garden Grove's population is eighty-four thousand.
1961: Garden Grove Community Church, forerunner of Crystal Cathedral, is established.
1963: Garden Grove resident Scott Carpenter orbits the earth in the Aurora 7 Mercury space capsule. He was the second American to orbit the earth, following John Glenn. Carpenter, who died in 2013, was also a pioneer in underwater exploration, spending twenty-eight days underwater in the Sealab in 1965.
1964: Realignment of major north–south streets in Garden Grove joins Euclid to Verano, Brookhurst to Wright, Magnolia to Cannery and Beach to Stanton. The shift of Euclid west bypasses the downtown area. A remnant of Euclid is renamed Main Street.
1964: Voters approve combining Garden Grove Union High District, Garden Grove (elementary) School District and Alamitos (elementary) School District into the new Garden Grove Unified School District. Unification takes effect in 1965.
1965: The Garden Grove Freeway is opened.
1968: New York senator Robert Kennedy appears in the Strawberry Festival parade and speaks at Bolsa Grande High Stadium. Three days later, he is assassinated in Los Angeles after winning the California Democratic presidential primary.
1968: The thirteen-story Tower of Hope at Chapman Avenue and Lewis Street opens on the campus of the Garden Grove Community Church.
1970: Garden Grove's population is 122,524.
1970: *Hour of Power* TV broadcasts by Reverend Robert Schuller begin.
1970: *Orange County Evening News* ceases daily publication. It goes to three times a week and then two.
1971: Protests against dress code occur in local schools. The code is abandoned after school board election results in the seating of candidates opposed to the code.
1973: After disturbances at Garden Grove Park, the Strawberry Festival is moved to Village Green Park in the downtown area.
1973: Voters in the GGUSD decide to split the district boundaries among three neighboring college districts instead of establishing a Garden Grove

Community College or affiliating with one college district. West of Euclid joined the Coast Community College District (Golden West College, Orange Coast College and Coastline Community College), and east went to the Rancho Santiago district (Santa Ana College). West Garden Grove is in the North Orange County system (Cypress and Fullerton colleges).
1974: The Santiago High School softball team wins the CIF crown, the first team section title for any local school.
1975: Saigon falls to North Vietnamese troops, ending the Vietnam War. Many thousands of refugees flee the country, and many of those eventually locate in the Garden Grove–Westminster area, creating two "Little Saigons."
1978: The Pacifica High School football team advances to the CIF Southern Section final, losing to El Modena, 20–6. It was the first local school to make it to the football finals since 1945.
1979: The renovated Gem Theater opens for live stage performances.
1980: Garden Grove's population is 125,900.
1981: Crystal Cathedral opens in Garden Grove.
1983: The *Garden Grove Journal* is founded.
1984: The Olympic torch run passes through Garden Grove.
1985: The fourteen-story Princess Alicante hotel opens at Chapman Avenue and Harbor Boulevard, the first of what would eventually become ten more mid- and high-rise hotels serving the tourists visiting nearby Disneyland and the Anaheim Convention Center.
1986: Bolsa Grande High School wins the first CIF football championship for a local school.
1990: Garden Grove's population is 142,965.
1990: A Mediterranean fruit fly infestation leads to the controversial aerial spraying of insecticide across Garden Grove.
1994: Pacifica High's boys' basketball team, coached by Bob Becker, wins the CIF Southern Section championship and advances to the state title game before losing.
1994: Bruce Broadwater is elected mayor. He goes on to serve longer than any other mayor in city history.
1996: Garden Grove celebrates its fifty years as a city with a party on Main Street in the city's original center.
1996: Garden Grove native Curt Pringle is elected speaker of the state assembly. He serves for one year.
1997: The Pacifica High School softball team not only wins the CIF Southern Section title but also is declared state and national champions by softball publications.

1999: A winter storm spreads thick snow-like hail across Garden Grove, enough to allow locals to make "hail-men" and throw "hail-balls."
2000: Garden Grove's population is 165,162.
2004: One-time Garden Grove resident Adam Gadahn is charged with treason for his association with Al-Quaeda terrorists. He is still at large.
2006: Garden Grove Unified School District is awarded the Broad Prize as the best urban school district in the United States.
2007–08: A proposal to build a huge casino on Harbor Boulevard in cooperation with some members of the Gabrielino tribe eventually is voted down by the Garden Grove City Council, with many members of the Vietnamese community opposed to the project, citing concerns about gambling addiction.
2007: Garden Grove native Steve Fossett is killed when his plane crashes in Nevada. Fossett was a famous businessman and explorer who held 116 records in five sports, including being the first person to fly nonstop around the world in a balloon. Fossett was also an accomplished skier and mountain climber. He was reported missing in September 2007 during a solo airplane flight across the Nevada desert; his remains were not found until more than a year later.
2008: Garden Grove resident Michael Monsoor is awarded the Medal of Honor posthumously for his heroism in 2006 as a Navy SEAL. While serving in Iraq, he threw himself on a live grenade to save his comrades.
2009: Garden Grove native Steve Martin hosts the Oscars. He would go on to win an honorary Oscar in 2013. Martin attended local schools, including Rancho Alamitos and Garden Grove high schools, graduating in 1963. He won a talent contest at an early Strawberry Festival and worked at Disneyland and Knott's Berry Farm while attending local schools and Santa Ana College. He later transferred to Long Beach State and also studied at UCLA.
2010: Garden Grove's population is 170,883.
2010: Garden Grove High wins the CIF Southern Section football title, the second in local school district history. The Argonauts will be finalists in 2009, 2012 and 2013. Star Josh Webb is named CIF Player of the Year and Orange County Football Player of the Year. He scores the winning points with somersaults into the end zone in the closing moments of the game.
2011: Garden Grove native Bert Blyleven is inducted into the Baseball Hall of Fame. Blyleven, a starting pitcher, won 287 games in the major leagues in a career that ran from 1970 to 1992. He played for the Minnesota Twins, Pittsburgh Pirates, Cleveland Indians and California Angels. He was a graduate of Santiago High School.

2013: Garden Grove's population is estimated to be 174,000 people.
2013: The Roman Catholic Diocese of Orange purchases the Crystal Cathedral, renaming it Christ Cathedral. The former Crystal Cathedral congregation relocates to the nearby campus of St. Callistus Church and is renamed Shepherd's Grove.
2014: The hotel district along Harbor Boulevard in Garden Grove is rebranded as the Grove District of the Anaheim Resort area.
2014: Construction begins on the Great Wolf Water Resort hotel on Harbor Boulevard, including a six-hundred-room hotel, conference and retail space. Completion is scheduled for 2016.

Appendix II

PROMINENT GARDEN GROVE PERSONALITIES

STEVE MARTIN is a famous TV and film actor, writer, comedian and musician. He is arguably Garden Grove's most famous "native son." Born in Texas, his family moved to Inglewood and then to Garden Grove. He attended Lampson (now Ralston) Intermediate School, Rancho Alamitos High School and Garden Grove High School. The 1963 graduating class of GGHS was indeed star-studded. In addition to Martin, the departing seniors included John McEuen of the Nitty Gritty Dirt Band ("Mr. Bojangles"); Bill (later Basil) Poledouris, an Emmy-winning musical composer who wrote scores for dozens of films and TV shows; and Kathy Westmoreland, an opera star, a pop singer and (reportedly) a romantic partner of Elvis Presley. The class of '63 is also noted for having received more college scholarships than any other high school in California.

BERT BLYLEVEN was a major-league baseball pitcher elected to the Hall of Fame in 2011. He's still in fifth place on the all-time strikeout list. He was a graduate of Santiago High School.

NORM JOHNSON was an NFL placekicker (mostly for the Seattle Seahawks). A two-time All-Pro, he's tenth all-time in league scoring. He was a graduate of Pacifica High School.

STEVE FOSSETT was a famed adventurer and businessman. He was the first man to make a nonstop flight around the world in a balloon. Fossett was reported missing in September 2007 while flying a private plane over the Nevada desert and was declared dead in 2008. His remains were found later that year. Born in Tennessee, he grew up in Garden Grove and was a member of the GGHS Class of 1962.

Michael Monsoor was a Navy SEAL awarded the Medal of Honor in 2008 for heroism by throwing himself on a grenade in 2006.

Tibor "Ted" Rubin is a Medal of Honor winner for heroism during the Korean War. A Hungarian-born Holocaust survivor, Rubin joined the U.S. Army in gratitude for being liberated and served in the Korean War. Not only did he fight bravely in combat, but once captured by Chinese Communists, he also worked tirelessly to assist his fellow POWs, sneaking out of the prison camp to steal food from enemy supplies to feed his comrades and otherwise caring for them. He received the MOH from President George W. Bush in 2005.

Nicole Brown Simpson married former football star O.J. Simpson in 1985; the two divorced in 1992. She was murdered in 1994 and her ex-husband arrested, but he was acquitted in the "Trial of the Century."

Adam Gadahn is wanted for treason for supporting the Al-Qaeda terrorist group.

Curt Pringle was speaker of the state assembly and later mayor of Anaheim.

Troy Polamalu is a star defensive player for the Pittsburgh Steelers of the NFL.

Mary Decker (Slaney) is an international track star who held six world records and was named Sportswoman of the Year in 1983. She famously tripped and fell in the three-thousand-meter event in the 1984 Olympic games in Los Angeles.

Robert H. Schuller founded the Crystal Cathedral and was host of the *Hour of Power* television broadcasts.

Gary Hall Sr. was a world-class swimmer who competed in the 1968, 1972 and 1976 Olympic games, winning a total of two silver and one bronze medals.

Ed Carruthers was a high jumper who won a bronze medal in the 1968 Olympic games. He was a teacher at Bolsa Grande High School when he competed.

Gary Davidson helped found the American Basketball Association, World Hockey Association and World Football League.

Scott Carpenter is one of the original seven Mercury astronauts, and he orbited the earth in Liberty 7 in 1963.

Amanda Freed is a softball pitcher who played on the U.S. gold medal Olympic team in 2004.

Alonzo Gerry Cook was the founding father of Garden Grove.

H. Louis Lake was the first mayor of Garden Grove.

Appendix III

PLACE NAMES AND LANDMARKS IN GARDEN GROVE

CHRIST CATHEDRAL, LEWIS AND CHAPMAN. Originally the Crystal Cathedral, this glass sanctuary is famous worldwide for its architecture. Set in a campus of other modern buildings, it is soon to be the center of Catholic life in Orange County.

MAIN STREET. Consisting of two blocks in the original central business district of the community, some historic buildings here are over one hundred years old. Special attractions include Kaye's Kitchen, Doug's Downtown Grill and the Gem Theatre, a one-time cinema now devoted to live musical comedy. Next to the Gem is the Festival Amphitheater, hosting the Shakespeare Orange County. Main Street and the surrounding area is known as downtown.

BROOKHURST STREET AND CHAPMAN AVENUE. This is the biggest shopping area of the city, composed of the Promenade center on the north of Chapman and the Pavilion Plaza on the south. It includes a sixteen-screen Regal Cinema complex, a Walmart department store, Ross Dress for Less, Marshall's, Party City, 24-Hour Fitness, PetSmart and other stores and services, including three banks and a half dozen eateries. It is sometimes called the Plaza or Uptown.

WEST GARDEN GROVE. Joined to the rest of the city by a narrow strip along Garden Grove Boulevard, West Garden Grove is the most affluent section of town. The main commercial strip is along Valley View Street, which includes banks, restaurants, supermarkets and office buildings.

Grove District/Anaheim Resort. That's the recently added name to the hotel and restaurant cluster along Harbor Boulevard at Chapman Avenue. Garden Grove and Anaheim have teamed up to promote tourism all along Harbor after years of rivalry.

Garden Grove High School. The oldest school campus in Garden Grove, GGHS traces its history back to 1921, although most of the present structures were built much later. Two buildings are WPA New Deal projects, and the Heritage Hall is a reconstruction of the main classroom edifice wrecked in the 1933 Long Beach Earthquake, in which one student was killed by falling debris. The campus includes a 5,000-capacity football stadium and a 1,500-seat auditorium.

Stanley Ranch and Museum. This historic village on Euclid Street just south of Chapman Avenue features lovingly restored or re-created buildings from the village and town eras of Garden Grove. Operated by the Garden Grove Historical Society, the site is open for tours on the first and third Sundays of the month at 1:30 p.m.

Buena-Clinton. Once derided as "the worst slum in Orange County," this area near Buena and Clinton Streets south of Westminster Avenue at the city's southeastern edge has been rehabilitated and is served by a city-operated family and youth center, as well as an outpost of the Boys and Girls Club of Garden Grove.

Pacific Electric right of way. This now-abandoned rail route runs like a diagonal scar through the city from northwest to southeast. Owned by the Orange County Transportation Authority, it's being considered as a possible route for a trolley or streetcar line.

Garden Grove Auto Center, along Trask Avenue from Euclid Street to Gilbert Street, parallel to the Garden Grove Freeway. Begun in the early 1980s, the center houses car dealerships for Chevrolet, Hyundai, Nissan, Scion, Toyota and Volkswagen. In the 1960s, new car dealerships were clustered along Garden Grove Boulevard and Brookhurst Street. Gone now are places to buy Studebakers, Dodges, Audis, Chryslers, Ramblers and

Mercurys. When it was a tradition for new car models to be unveiled to the public each fall, the sky was filled with sweeping searchlights summoning locals to view the latest from Detroit.

Magnolia Memorial Park, on Magnolia Street south of Chapman Avenue. Founded in the 1880s as a cemetery for the Westminster colony to the south, this graveyard contains the mortal remains of many area pioneers, including some who fought in the Civil War. Now privately operated, it was a public cemetery for many years until sold by the county.

Town & Country Estates. Garden Grove's first gated community is located on Gilbert Street near Orangewood, featuring large houses on huge lots, with swimming pools and tennis courts. Nicole Brown Simpson's family lived there before moving to Dana Hills. It was once considered the "Beverly Hills of Garden Grove."

Parks of prominence. These include the Village Green (originally Euclid Park, the city's oldest park) in the downtown area, which hosts the annual Strawberry Festival; Civic Center Park at Euclid Street and Stanford Avenue, which includes ponds, waterfalls and lots of waterfowl; Eastgate Park in West Garden Grove, a locale for free summer concerts; and Garden Grove Park, the city's biggest (Westminster Avenue at Deodara Street), which features a gymnasium, dog park, skate spot and the water-themed Atlantis Play Center.

Little Saigon. There are actually two "Little Saigons" in Garden Grove. The larger, better-known Vietnamese business district along Bolsa Avenue between Beach and Brookhurst Streets includes a small slice of Garden Grove, as most of the area is in Westminster. A second, smaller shopping area by the same name is in the area of Brookhurst Street and Westminster Avenue. Slowly developing in the same area is a neighborhood of Arab and Moslem residents (primarily from Egypt and the rest of the Middle East) clustering around the Islamic Society of Orange County's campus on Thirteenth Street, west of Brookhurst Street.

Koreatown. This is the Korean business district (sometimes called "Little Seoul") along Garden Grove Boulevard between Brookhurst Street and Beach Boulevard. It was originally the Garden Square, home to the first shopping center in the city and one of the first in Orange County. Many of the original buildings have been replaced with modern, enclosed mall-like structures. Longtime residents remember when that area was home to the All-American Market, the chain that became Albertson's; Judkins Music, where many youngsters bought their first musical instruments and learned how to play; and C.R. Anthony, a small department store.

LOARA STREET. It's tucked away off Chapman Avenue, but this road (across from Mark Twain School) is adorned with huge, multimillion-dollar homes that look a little out of place among the low-slung ranch houses that still comprise most of the local housing stock. If you want to impress the folks back home with how affluent Garden Grove is, send them a photo of this neighborhood.

KIWANISLAND. This large private park is tucked away a block behind Garden Grove Boulevard. Operated by the local Kiwanis organization, it includes a large patio area with kitchen, an enclosed clubhouse, an outdoor amphitheater and a stage. It's landscaped with water features and trees. It stands next to a major campus of the Boys and Girls Club of Garden Grove.

Appendix IV

GONE BUT STILL REMEMBERED

BELISLE'S RESTAURANT. Located at Harbor and Chapman, this eatery was famous for its huge portions, such as a brownie the size of a meatloaf. It was a favorite of pro football players when the Los Angeles Rams played in Anaheim. The site is now occupied by an Outback Steakhouse.

GOLD STREET. A one-time barn at Beach and Garden Grove Boulevards, it became a restaurant and nightclub in the 1960s, hosting such acts as Sonny and Cher. The land is now occupied by a center including a service station, fast-food outlet and a car wash.

KIDS' HAVEN. Situated at West Street and Chapman Avenue, this spot is not completely gone, except in terms of its former use. It's now a flood control basin operated by the County of Orange, but it was once a Tom Sawyer–esque venue for camping and fishing, with recreation provided by the Izaak Walton League. It's no longer open to the public.

GREENBRIER INN AND GARDEN GROVE SANITARIUM. This was a rehab center and adjacent hotel on Garden Grove Boulevard at Nelson Street. Described in detail in Chapter 7.

GARDEN GROVE DEPOT. Located west of what is now Main Street in what is presently the parking lot of the Home Depot, this stop along the Pacific Electric railway was the community's chief connection to the outside world before freeways and major highways. Packinghouses grew up around the depot.

HASTER AIR FIELD. Off Westminster Boulevard and west of Magnolia Street, this was operated by the U.S. Navy for several months during World War II. It is now the site of Garden Grove Park and Bolsa Grande High School.

STRAWBERRY FIELDS. The biggest was located at Chapman Avenue and Euclid Street. Previously an orange grove, the land was developed as the Heritage housing project in the 1990s. The last strawberry field was at Hazard Avenue and Euclid Street. A condo project built in 2012 now occupies that location.

BOB'S BIG BOY. For young Grovers in the 1950s, '60s and '70s, the two Bob's restaurants (one at Chapman and Harbor, currently a Coco's, and one at Gilbert Street and Garden Grove Boulevard, now gone) were the place to go on Friday nights after football and basketball games. It was the equivalent of the "malt shop" for baby boomer kids.

DENNO'S RECORDS. This record shop in the Orange County Plaza (Chapman and Brookhurst) thronged with teens in the time of Elvis and the Beatles. It had a promotional deal with KWIZ in Santa Ana that kept customers coming in, and live performances by talent like the Beach Boys didn't hurt either.

THE JOLLY KNIGHT. This classic restaurant on Garden Grove Boulevard and Newland Street was the high-class eatery for the community through the early 1980s. Decorated in a faux-English motif with lots of brass and red leather, it was famous for its steaks and piano bar. The site is now a housing project.

OTHER MEMORABLE RESTAURANTS included the Imperial/Salvatore's (not far from the Jolly Knight), the Pink Spot (drive-up burger place where the Wendy's is now located on Chapman, east of Brookhurst) and the Copper Penny (Orange County Plaza).

THE ALAMITOS AREA in the northwestern section of the main body of Garden Grove is now largely forgotten as a distinct geographical area. The former Alamitos Friends Church (Magnolia and Chapman) is now Garden Grove Friends. The last remnant of the name in Garden Grove is Alamitos

Intermediate School at Lampson Avenue and Dale Street. *Alamitos* means "little cottonwoods" in Spanish.

OTHER FORGOTTEN GEOGRAPHY for Garden Grove includes Sun Gardens (Garden Grove Boulevard and Dale Street), Berryfield (Chapman and Brookhurst, also known as Harperville), Berrydale (near Westminster Avenue and Fairview), 88 Acres (south of Garden Grove Boulevard, east of Brookhurst Street, also known as Sunnyside Gardens), Colonia La Paz (a Mexican American community northeast of Euclid Street and Westminster Avenue), Garden Acres (Garden Grove Boulevard and Magnolia Street) and Gospel Swamp (near Ward Street), so-called because of the outdoor church services held in the wetlands at the extreme southern edges of what's now the city limits. Most of what was then called Gospel Swamp is now within the borders of Fountain Valley and Huntington Beach.

FLAG STOPS on the railways included Buaro (Seventeenth/Westminster at Harbor), Cordinez (Magnolia and Orangewood), Mesto (Brookhurst and Chapman) and Metate (Nelson Street north of Garden Grove Boulevard).

RADIO. Beginning in the late 1950s, KGGK broadcast from tiny studios at Orange County Plaza, changed its call letters to KTBT and eventually moved to the city in Orange. The format was easy listening rock as KORJ and then country music (KIK-FM). Even though the offices and transmitter were located in Orange, it was still licensed to Garden Grove until the owners sold the frequency rights (94.3) to a Spanish-language broadcaster based in Los Angeles.

THE ORIGINAL CITY HALL. Built in 1923 on Acacia Parkway as Washington Grammar School (later Fitz Intermediate), this building was eventually closed to students because it did not meet state earthquake standards. When Garden Grove incorporated in 1956, the new municipal government moved into the structure. It was torn down in the 1990s when a move was made into a newer, more modern three-story building several blocks away. The site is now occupied by the Acacia Adult Day Care Center.

THE KOREAN FESTIVAL and parade was held annually in the Koreatown district along Garden Grove Boulevard between Brookhurst and Gilbert Streets, usually in October. After twenty-nine years, the festival was moved to Buena Park in 2013 in response to a growing Korean American community in that city.

MARMAC'S. This was a popular West Garden Grove restaurant and watering hole at Stanford Avenue and Knott Street in the 1960s through the '90s. It is now the Garden Room banquet hall.

PRONTO MARKET. Located at West Street and Chapman Avenue, this was one of the first in a convenience store chain that would morph into Trader Joe's, a popular upscale market. Ironically, Trader Joe's now refuses to locate in Garden Grove, citing demographic issues.

GARDEN GROVE BOOK STORE. Originally located on Euclid/Main Streets in the downtown area in the early 1960s, it later moved to Chapman Avenue (across from the Orange County Plaza). Like most independent bookstores, it fell victim to competition from chain booksellers such as B. Dalton, Waldenbooks and Crown Books. They, in turn, have been replaced by giant bookstores like Barnes & Noble, which is now suffering from competition from online purchasing and e-books.

PUBLICATIONS. The local print media included newspapers like the *Post* (1969), *Pony Express and Rocket* (both mid-1950s), the *Grove* (mid-1990s) and a magazine, *Garden Country* (early 1980s).

Appendix V

GARDEN GROVE MYTHS AND LEGENDS

The most persistent local legend is that Disneyland could have been located in Garden Grove. While Walt might have passed through on his search for a site, he was looking for a city with a location on the route of the Santa Ana Freeway. In 1955, when the park opened, Garden Grove was still an unincorporated town with no direct freeway access.

Another local legend has Garden Grove city fathers in the mid-1960s rejecting The City shopping center because of a reluctance to help pay for sewer costs. Officials in Orange deny this, saying that the land was already within their city limits when the proposal was first put forth. One fun fact: the original name for the development (later named the Block and now the Outlets at Orange) was Four City, reflecting its proximity to Anaheim, Orange, Santa Ana and Garden Grove.

Millions in gold bullion in Garden Grove? The story goes like this: an elderly couple living on Stanford Avenue between Brookhurst and Gilbert Streets keeps bars of gold bullion under the wooden floor of their house. Every time a new police chief is appointed, the couple politely calls on him to advise him of the treasure so he can assign extra security to the area. It's probably not true, as three police chiefs deny the story, but, on the other hand, wouldn't they?

Black gold under our feet? Could there be a big lake of dead dinosaur juice under our streets and homes? Several attempts have been made to drill exploratory wells, and as recently as 1988, Chevron Oil bought up oil rights and sought city permission to sink a well, but the permit was rejected by the city council on a 3–2 vote after a public outcry. Oil down there? Could be.

There aren't too many buildings still standing which are old enough to justify a good, red-blooded ghost story in Garden Grove, but we're not totally devoid of otherworldly tales. "Jasper" is the name given to the good-natured ghost who supposedly dwelt at the old Girls Club building on Garden Grove Boulevard. An unnamed spook was reported in the Gem Theatre on Main Street by some actors, but having a ghost is a tradition in many theaters. At Garden Grove High School, the shade of Elizabeth Pollard, killed in the 1933 quake, is said to roam the halls of the Heritage Hall building, where she met her premature demise.

Appendix VI
ALMOST GARDEN GROVE

Like many cities, Garden Grove has its own roster of dashed dreams and could-have-beens. Here are some of the most prominent.

An enclosed shopping mall. Plans to enclose the Orange County Plaza were put forth in the 1950s and early '80s but were never carried out. An enclosed mall including an attached hotel and ice-skating rink was proposed in the early 1980s on the site of the old Greenbrier Inn. Instead, condos were built.

Garden Grove Community College. The local area was one of the few remaining areas not part of a community college district. A proposal to create a Garden Grove district and build a two-year school here (possibly on the site of Garden Grove High) was floated but rejected in the early 1970s. The city's college territory was eventually carved up among three neighboring districts.

Light rail. In 1984, Orange County voters rejected a sales tax increase that would have built a rapid transit train line along the old Pacific Electric right of way through Garden Grove with stations on Chapman Avenue, Euclid Street and Harbor Boulevard. The line would have connected Santa Ana to Buena Park and served as a "starter" for a larger countywide system.

Chapman University. One of America's fastest-rising private colleges, Chapman University twice considered locations in Garden Grove. In the

1980s, the city tried to lure the school to the vacant lots at Euclid Street and Garden Grove Boulevard to build its planned law school. Instead, a site across the street from the college in Orange was chosen. More recently, Chapman sought to buy the Crystal Cathedral and grounds for a planned medical school but was outbid by the Diocese of Orange.

High-Rises. Office towers of ten stories or higher were planned for the west end of Orange County Plaza in the 1960s and the land at Beach and Garden Grove Boulevard, but they never went any further…or higher.

Pro sports. When Angels owner Gene Autry was wrangling with Anaheim over improvements in the stadium, he told reporters he was looking at sites for a new facility in Santa Ana, Fullerton and Garden Grove. In the 1990s, when city planners were speculating on the future of Harbor Boulevard, one report suggested that a minor-league hockey team (and rink) would be a good attraction for the area. The closest Garden Grove ever came to professional sports (aside from athletes staying at local hotels) were the polo matches on grounds near Gilbert Street and Garden Grove Boulevard. According to local legend, celebrities such as Will Rogers and Douglas Fairbanks kept their ponies there.

SOURCES

The author gratefully acknowledges the valuable resources listed below:

Brigandi, Phil. *Orange County Place Names A to Z*. San Diego, CA: Sunbelt Publications, 2006.

City of Garden Grove, historical records and photographs.

Doig, Leroy. *The City of Garden Grove*. Santa Ana, CA: Pioneer Press, 1976.

———. *The Town of Garden Grove*. Santa Ana, CA: Pioneer Press, 1966.

———. *The Village of Garden Grove*. Santa Ana, CA: Pioneer Press, 1962.

Garden Grove Historical Society newsletters, 1971–76. Also various other documents, sources and other assistance.

Garden Grove Journal, various articles.

Garden Grove News (also *Daily News*, *Orange County Evening News*, *Orange County News*), various articles.

Head, H.C. *The History of Garden Grove.* Garden Grove, CA: Garden Grove News, 1939.

Los Angeles Times, various articles.

Marge Swenson, interviews and conversations.

Orange County Register, various articles.

Orangecountytribune.com, various posts.

INDEX

W

Z

ABOUT THE AUTHOR

Jim Tortolano is a professor of journalism and mass communications at Golden West College in Huntington Beach, California.

He has an extensive background in newspapers, having served as a writer and/or editor for the *Long Beach Press-Telegram*, *Fontana Herald-News*, *Orange County Evening News*, *Huntington Beach Independent*, *Garden Grove Journal* and *Los Angeles Times*.

He's lived in Garden Grove since 1960 and is married to Marilyn Lewis, whose family moved to Garden Grove in 1957. They both graduated from Garden Grove High School in 1971. He was active in student government and journalism at GGHS.

Jim has an associate arts degree from Golden West College and a bachelor's degree from California State University–Long Beach. He is the founding editor and former owner of the *Garden Grove Journal*, which was sold to Freedom Communications in 2013.

In addition to his careers in journalism and education, he has been active in the Garden Grove Downtown Business Association and Shakespeare

Orange County and served seven years in the California State Military Reserve in the public affairs office of the Fortieth Infantry Division Support Brigade/Regional Support Command South.

He operates a local history website, www.orangecountytribune.com, and is also the author of a novel, *No Justice*. He lives in Garden Grove with Marilyn and one good dog and one bad cat.

www.ingramcontent.com/pod-product-compliance
Lightning Source LLC
Chambersburg PA
CBHW060809100426
42813CB00004B/999
* 9 7 8 1 5 4 0 2 1 2 7 1 9 *